Save Yourself!

Six Pathways to Achievement in the Age of Change

Robert D. Gilbreath

McGraw-Hill, Inc.

New York   St. Louis   San Francisco   Auckland   Bogotá
Caracas   Hamburg   Lisbon   London   Madrid
Mexico   Milan   Montreal   New Delhi   Paris
San Juan   São Paulo   Singapore
Sydney   Tokyo   Toronto

To Lt. Col. Joseph A. Levy,
U.S. Army Special Forces, 1971–72.
Thanks for helping me save myself.

Gilbreath, Robert D. (Robert Dean), date.
    Save yourself! : Six Pathways to Achievement in the Age of Change /
Robert D. Gilbreath.
        p.   cm.
    Includes index.
    ISBN 0-07-023462-0 :
    1. Organizational change.   2. Success.   3. Creative ability in busi-
ness.   I. Title.
HD58.8.G54   1990
650.1—dc20
                                                                    90-6659
                                                                    CIP

    2 3 4 5 6 7 8 9 0   DOC/DOC   9 5 4 3 2 1

ISBN   0-07-023462-0

The sponsoring editor for this book was James H. Bessent, Jr.,
the editing supervisor was Alfred Bernardi, the designer was
Naomi Auerbach, and the production supervisor was Pamela
Pelton. It was set in Baskerville by McGraw-Hill's Professional Publish-
ing composition unit.

Printed and bound by R. R. Donnelley & Sons Company.

A sixty-minute audio program to accompany this book is now available. Ask
for it at your local bookstore or phone toll-free 1-800-2-MCGRAW.

Contents

Preface

A voice came to me in the middle of the night and asked me to write this book. It wasn't a dream or a vision, but more like an information-age epiphany. It was two in the morning and I was in the CNN studio in Atlanta staring into a camera. I was appearing on their "Newsnight" program as part of a book tour promoting my most recent work. In a live broadcast throughout the United States, Europe, and Asia, I was being interviewed about the business impacts of change. After a few minutes of discussion the call-in phone lines were open to viewers and that voice was in my earpiece.

"I'm working for a company that's just been bought, and I need to know how to protect my job. What can I do to save myself?" I was taken aback, so used to dealing with corporate change, culture change, and business transformation as a topic that I was unprepared to give individual advice to the very people affected the most. More questions from other callers followed. "My division is going down the tubes and I've got the feeling I'm the only one who cares"; "I want to make changes around the office, but my boss is resisting"; "No one knows what the new computer system will mean"; "The parts I've made all my life are going to be made in Mexico"; "I'm being _____ and I don't know what to do." For the blank in the last sentence, substitute "laid off," "promoted," "transferred," "outsourced," "decentralized," "automated," "off-shored," "attritioned," and any other current euphemism for personal job change.

The CNN show was the first of over 50 television and radio

appearances on my schedule. Over and over, in city after city I heard the same message: Everything is changing and I'm caught up in it. What do I do to save myself? Now, after more than three years of speeches, lectures, and consulting assignments (all devoted to the subject of business change) throughout the United States and in more than twenty foreign countries, I'm ready to give some answers. Not new corporate strategies, not new organizational theories, and not simply another voice in the chorus that's been crying, Change is coming! Change is coming! I'm ready to tell you *what to do in a changing business world*. What steps to take, what techniques to use, what to watch out for. How to survive and succeed. How to save yourself when change is either around the corner or on top of you.

I'll share what I've learned in factories being automated, utilities being deregulated, banks being consolidated, stores being sold, government agencies being cut back, insurance companies reorganizing, airlines merging, subsidiaries spinning off, and massive information systems being installed. I'll include what I've learned from board chairpersons, chief executive officers, chief information officers, presidents, directors, and manufacturing engineers; from sales people, teachers, hospital administrators, shop supervisors, union stewards, and armies of white-collar workers lined up behind computer terminals, service counters, and drafting tables. You won't hear all their stories, but rather, my synthesis of what their stories mean. You'll hear echoes of their complaints, fears, hopes, and challenges. You'll receive the net result in an organized, concise way. One that you can put to use easily, quickly, and effectively. You'll learn the fundamental skills needed to make it in a world under transition, the world in which we all work.

I'll also tell you what can go wrong, and why. You'll be able to spot changing situations instantly, prepare for their impacts on you, and reconnect with meaningful, rewarding work. But the rules for such work may be new and unfamiliar to you now. I'll make them understandable. Above all, you'll be able to discern between rules that worked in the age of stability, the past, and the ones that are absolutely essential for the age of change, our age.

The first step is important. You've got to accept the fact that the way to succeed in the past may be the way that leads to frustration, failure, and permanent damage to your well-being today. All these changes—competition, globalization, information technology, deregulation, quality and service campaigns, productivity pushes, mergers, changing demographics, and more—have combined to make our working conditions and concerns very different. *A new world of work requires new rules and new survival techniques.*

So expect some surprising or even upsetting messages here. I can't make change any less threatening or powerful, and I can't play down its reach. Everybody either *is* being tested by it or *soon will be*. I want you to pass the test. I want you to win by winning *through* change, not by fighting it or ignoring it. It won't go away. If you know the new rules and practice the new techniques, you'll protect your job, your sanity, and your future. If you don't, you could end up a victim.

The focus of this book is on six central, critical abilities which I call *Pathways*. Once mastered, they work together to help you triumph under the conditions we all face now and will continue to face for the foreseeable future. If you are among the millions of employees and managers in the middle of change or in its path, you'll benefit from the key skills contained here. You'll put them to work immediately, and you'll see almost instant payoff and protection. This book is for you, the person who cares about his or her job, knows that change is the rule and not the exception anymore, and wants to take active steps to respond to it. The tricks you learn might not be called on right away, but when the time comes, when you're taking the bus or the train or driving your car to work and wondering what's going to happen next and what it means for you, you will remember them. You'll be able to *save yourself*. And I'll have answered the question that came in the middle of the night, the one that has haunted me since.

ROBERT D. GILBREATH

About the Author

As the president of Change Management Associates in
Atlanta, Robert D. Gilbreath has served as a consultant to
major corporations and governments throughout the world,
among them General Motors, Kraft Foods, Johnson &
Johnson, Aetna, Phillips Petroleum (Norway), the Parliament
of the United Kingdom, Carnation, and Chiyoda (Japan).
He is the author of three management books, including
Forward Thinking (McGraw-Hill, 1987), and has written for
leading periodicals, appeared on scores of radio and
television programs, and lectured at leading universities
around the world. Gilbreath is also the creator of more than
200 management and business seminars, which have been
presented in over 20 countries. He is currently appearing as
the expert commentator on the AMA's *Winning Through
Change* videos.

Introduction:
Welcome to Crunch Time

If you're feeling some anxiety and concern about your job, your company, and your future, you're not alone. These are common symptoms in our changing, jerking, spasmodic business world. They reflect major transformations that have been under way for some time and from which no company and no individual can escape. Business is getting tougher, work is more demanding, and uncertainty is rampant. Fasten your seatbelts. The ride is just beginning.

If people can suffer schizophrenia and sudden mood swings, so can businesses and entire industries. The reasons are now all too familiar: competition, deregulation, technology, demographics, and globalization. These and many other "change drivers" are turning the once predictable, secure, and even enjoyable world of work upside down. And like Casey Stengel once said, "The future ain't what it used to be." General Electric's chairman Jack Welch has labeled the next ten years the "white-knuckle decade." Thousands of workers,

supervisors and middle managers let go by his policies might
phrase it differently. At the very top, few, if any, worried
about saving them. They had to *save themselves*.

America Is an Unsafe
Place to Work

The early part of this century was dominated by risks at
work—getting mangled in the machinery, dropping from ex-
haustion in sweatshops, being poisoned by industrial chemi-
cals. But don't think that just because you don't work in a
sausage factory or a garment garret that you're now safe.
The risks have changed, but they haven't gone away. We've
got new ones now.

We're no longer mangled by machinery—we're mangled
by mergers. We're not poisoned, we're "repositioned" to
lower-paying jobs with fewer benefits and lessened security.
We're not made lame in the factory, we're laid off in a "funds
management" manipulation.

No, we no longer work in sweatshops, we work in
"fearshops"—waiting for the next shoe to drop and sweating
bullets until it does. The most dangerous occupations aren't
mining and steelmaking—they're white-collar jobs, middle
management, sales, production, staff, service.

Forget the old statistics—*the most dangerous job is the one
you have*, no matter what it is. The most important person,
the one you should be fighting to save, is you.

Any time two or more idiots can scrape up enough nerve
to convince a moneylender they know best, your entire company is in for new ownership, and you're in jeopardy. Any
time a greedy manipulator sees more profit in turning your
organization into salable parts, the glue that binds your corporate culture suddenly loses its hold. When thieves steal a
new Lincoln or Mercedes and take it to a chop shop, a beautiful machine is cut up into replacement parts for the black
market. The same thing happens to companies. Only the
names are different—you don't go to a chop shop, you go

through a downsizing, a reorganization, a divestiture. Some parts get sold off, some get cut up, and some get trashed. And you're powerless to do anything about it. Until now.

Victims of Change

Victims of change are everywhere: steelworkers shut out of closed plants, taxi drivers with advanced degrees in psychology, government employees laboring under wage restrictions and over an increasingly unskilled work force, and managers facing twice as much work with half the staff and half the time to accomplish it...Or contingency workers with no benefits and part-time employment...Or even the successful survivors—the ones who must learn new jobs quickly, manage disgruntled or disenfranchised workers, and satisfy upper management that itself doesn't know what it wants. And those wants and demands are apt to change daily.

The Game Is Turmoil

One word best describes it: *Turmoil.* It's also the name of a video game in which objects, opponents, and challenges are thrown at the player at ever-increasing speed and in ever-greater numbers. The more creatures you destroy the faster their mutant replacements attack you. The sooner you learn the tricks the faster the tricks change, and the more exotic they become until you reach the inevitable conclusion and the end of the game. You crash, you give up, you become a victim. We are all playing a game of Turmoil. Boards of directors, senior executives, and top management have consultants, contingency funds, white knights, and golden parachutes to protect them. The rest of us aren't so fortunate. We're left to our wits, our courage, and our luck. And as with the video game, we've got to employ them at ever-increasing speed.

The Quick and the Dead

There is no standing still. You either move forward or down-ward. And moving forward means moving fast. None of us can afford slow, plodding, gradual accommodation to change or even advancement. The world is moving too quickly. We've got to go *fast-forward*. We've got to be smart and quick to survive and succeed, to *save ourselves*.

The chapters that follow are designed to help you do just that. In a systematic way, you'll learn how to adapt to the world in which you operate, how to detect change before it comes, how to find and solve problems quickly, how to be-come resourceful—using what you have to get what you need or want. And you'll discover the secrets of innovation within you and put them to use. You'll strengthen your natural tal-ents for change, learn how and when to respond to the busi-ness aliens and missiles hurled at you and how to lead others through the maze of change that characterizes our chaotic conditions. No person, no corporation, no union, and no professional association is providing a safety net if you should fall. You've got to *save yourself*. I will show you how.

Between a Rock and a Hard Place

Whether you're just entering the job market or are a veteran, whether you're a middle manager or an executive, you need new skills for this new world. The tricks and techniques that worked before are liable to kill you or, at a minimum, frus-trate and confuse you. Most of us are now caught between a rock and a hard place, between an irresistible force and an immovable object. The irresistible force is *change*—the new environments and the new rules. The immovable object is a stubborn combination of formal and unwritten rules, regula-tions, and standards that are left over from the old world. Or it's the reluctance or refusal of those above and below you to adapt. Either way, you're caught in the squeeze. *Crunch time* has begun.

What's So New? What's So Powerful?

Business commentators, myself included, have been noting dramatic shifts for several years. Increased competition is the most obvious one. I recall my plebe year at West Point and the dreaded boxing class every morning. When the first day of sparring came, I was fortunate enough to be paired in the ring with my best friend, Dan Jackson. We were supposed to lay into each other, really punch and really do damage. Jackson and I danced around a little and gave each other knowing winks. The message between us was clear: Cooperate and survive, play along, take it easy on me and I'll take it easy on you, we'll make it together. After two rounds of thinly disguised powder-puff pugilism, an unexpected blow landed on the side of my head and I fell to the canvas, unconscious. When I came to a minute later, I noticed Jackson, about ten feet away, on his back and knocked out cold. Standing above us was the boxing instructor, Mr. Joe.

Mr. Joe had seen through our act, snuck into the ring, and clobbered each of us from behind. "Nobody leaves this ring until I see a bloody face!" he screamed down at us. When Jackson and I wobbled to our feet, there was no knowing wink, no implied cooperation. All deals were off, it was a new match. We proceeded to beat the hell out of each other—with passion.

Who's Climbing Into Your Ring?

In case you haven't noticed, several Mr. Joes have stepped into our business ring and are clobbering us from behind.

They have changed the rules. American businesses used to be somewhat "gentlemanly," with opponents like General Motors, Chrysler, and Ford winking at each other and going along to get along. The competition was contrived, or at least benign. Now they know that no one leaves the ring unless he or his opponent has a bloody face.

Competition is fierce on two levels. Corporations are competing for market share, stock values, lower costs, higher profits, and simple survival. But individuals within those corporations are competing as well, with each other. Thanks to the baby boom there are just a lot more middle managers than middle-management positions. And top management is bent on eliminating more and more of those positions. Automation is making skilled work obsolete, and information systems are bypassing the traditional layers of management, making their futures suspect. Add to this mergers, acquisitions, and other "strategic alliances." The result is more work, fewer jobs, and more demands on those who still have them.

Now-ism

Don't be fooled by promises of strategic visions, long-term commitments, or a "future" with the company, the government, or the institution. These are myths from our parents' time. If there is a term for the atmosphere here it's *now-ism*, an exclusive interest in the present. Bosses, pressed for immediate results, are asking, "What are you doing for me NOW?" rather than, "What have you done in the past or what do you plan to accomplish in the future?"

Philosophers have long told us to release the past, not to worry about the future, just simply enjoy the present, the moment. American management has taken this to new extremes of absurdity. They talk about plans and long-term goals, but they don't really believe in them. Their "horizons" are the length of a conference table, their time frames the duration of a power lunch. They want theirs and they want it now. They remind me of the speculator who buys a parcel of land, runs out to see it as soon as the deed is in hand, and stands on it shouting, "Alright, damn it, start appreciating!"

Higher Stakes, Faster Times

There are exceptions, but they are more often in appearance than in reality. You can't bet your sanity, your security, or your future on exceptions. You've got to assume that loyalty is crumbling if not counterfeit and that the talk about professional development, potential, and career paths is just that— talk. You're playing Turmoil, and you can't rely on the rules that applied to Scrabble or Monopoly. With them you had all the time in the world, the rules were constant, and your opponents were known. If you lost, you lost some pride or play money. With Turmoil, when you lose you get disintegrated.

Most of us are being evaluated in real-time, continuously. We don't get a chance to take a make-up test or to pull our grades up next semester. We've got to do it now, now, now. We've got to move *fast-forward* or not move at all.

Just like the game Turmoil, as soon as you think you're secure, that you've got it figured out, the pressure doubles, the pace accelerates, the intensity is squared, and your opponents get fiercer. To stay in the game, you've got to have skills that make you smarter, more adaptive, and more alert, instantly. He or she who hesitates will be crunched.

Management Is Abandoning Ship

One of the most foolish ideas you can have is that someone somewhere up there in top management is concerned about you or cares about you or is acting in your long-term best interest. Perish the thought! Most top execs are as confused, harassed, and anxious as you are. Most are looking out for themselves and their buddies. Their personal advancement is not necessarily tied to you, to their group, or even to the company. They are playing Turmoil on an even larger scale.

By the thousands, they are looking over their shoulders at their own set of invading aliens: greenmail, foreign competitors, poison pills, golden handcuffs and parachutes, mergers, acquisitions, stock deals, budget cuts, early retirement, and the like. They have more powerful weapons and larger shields, but they're struggling to survive Turmoil too. If that means tossing you, your department, or your entire corporation off the mother ship or in front of the space invaders, you're gone.

Business Schizophrenia and Paranoia

Gone are the days when you were a part of an ongoing division, department, or even company. Gone is the security of professional associates, mentors, fatherly or motherly or big-brotherly supervisors. Gone are all associative bonds, even if your company stays the same. You're being reorganized, reclassified, refocused, retrained, merged, spun off, sold, reassigned, and retrofitted. You're being placed into temporary assignments, task forces, project teams—all churning and changing all the time.

You're working in joint ventures, strategic alliances, merged units, with acquired properties, with subcontractors and consultants. Who's "us" and who's "them" anymore? Who's friend and who's foe? *Sybil*, with her 21 personalities, is no longer just an old movie; it's contemporary business reality.

Start Identifying With Yourself

The net result is you can no longer identify yourself with or take comfort in a group, location, product, profession, skill, service, or set of relationships. They are leaves in the wind.

You must, therefore, start identifying with yourself. To save yourself you've got to vest yourself with skills that endure, withstand, and accommodate change.

Most people prefer a portable pension program they can take from job to job over one that ties them to a certain company. Likewise, you should start concentrating on a portable protection program—portable, transferrable, adaptive skills—not for when you retire, but so you can stay working, sane, and satisfied. The good news is that these aren't hard to come by. You've got most of them inside already. All you need to do is find them and start using them.

The sad truth, however, is that to get to these survival skills, most of us need to dig beneath a ton of accumulated, outdated, and dangerous truisms of the past that aren't true anymore. We've got to *unlearn* what we have been (and still are being) told about what it takes to succeed and learn what really succeeds today, in times of Turmoil.

The Old Rules Are Killing You

The acceleration of business change has one effect most people overlook. It's the obsolescence of wisdom as soon as it's gained. By the time you learn what works, it no longer works. The unfortunate part is that your management and the tools they use to manage were built on the last version of the rules. They're asking you to use yesterday's ways of thinking to survive today's challenges and threats.

Don't depend on them anymore. Rely on yourself to recognize what's current, what's effective. But before you can do that, you've got some housecleaning to do. You've got to get rid of the old rules.

Here are just a few of the most common and most damaging misconceptions about business today:

Do good work and you will be rewarded, sooner or later.

This is a leftover from the Puritan days. It's a dream. We know now that good work can just as well mean *more* work, being taken for granted, being ignored, or being held back because you're too valuable to promote. And we know that there is little chance that good work will even be noticed in the long run. No one above you stays long enough to notice.

Do what you're told.

That's easy to do when everything is stable and predictable. But now you're either not told at all or you're given conflicting commands and opposing expectations. Or there is absolutely no one to tell you what to do. You're told to increase quality and service and cut costs, to work harder but relax more in order to avoid stress, to satisfy the customer (who wants a discount) and to satisfy the boss (who wants all customers to pay full fare). One middle manager told me, "I've trained four bosses in the past year and a half and been given three new top priorities. Who's in charge?" No one is. Turmoil is in charge.

Concentrate on one thing—specialize.

No skill, technique, job assignment, or talent lasts forever. Specialization is a very risky course in times of change. What if your specialty is "outsourced," "offshored," automated, streamlined, sold, or otherwise zapped? You've bet on one horse and lost. What makes more sense is to concentrate on *skills* and *abilities* that work *under all conditions*, ones that you can transfer from assignment to assignment, place to place, job to job. Tie yourself to these skills, not to the momentary needs of your company or your situation.

A grateful boss will pull you upward.

Maybe, but only when he or she really needs you and can get you at no political or cultural cost. In other words, don't count on the benevolence of a superior. They can be transferred, retired, relocated, or "attritioned" themselves. They can fall out of favor in the continuous game of musical chairs now being played in business theaters everywhere, and you suffer along with them. If you need a rabbi, go to the synagogue. If you need a godfather, go to Las Vegas.

Experience pays off.

This rule has really been upended. Anyone over age 40 knows experience can be a major handicap. I've heard personnel directors and recruiters state a preference for young, green, "pliable" candidates. When job tasks have been automated, "dumbed down," and "deskilled," it doesn't take experience to handle them. It takes naiveté and trust. Experience means you have a mind. Many employers see that as dangerous.

But seriously, remember that job requirements change very frequently, knowledge does become obsolete, and the ability to adapt, respond, and reengage the work is paramount. Few corporate training departments and few universities teach this magic trick. You will learn it here.

Management knows best.

They know what's best for *them*, not necessarily what's best for you. And if it comes to a choice, don't expect them to risk anything on your behalf. Sure, some are competent and concerned. But many more are either incompetent or out for themselves, to hell with everyone else. Don't for a minute expect them to go beyond lip service to take actual, personal risks on behalf of those below. And don't think they know best because they're on top. They might know best according to the old rules, the ones that existed while *they* made it to the top. But that was before Mr. Joe stepped into the ring. Top management is struggling to save top management. You've got to *save yourself*.

The New Rules of Survival

Specific rules, techniques, and tricks are described in the remaining chapters in detail. But here I'd like to give you a few overarching rules—the ones you should keep in mind as you learn how to save yourself, how to move *fast-forward*, how to win at Turmoil.

The old rules don't apply.

You may still hear them. You may still be asked to conform to them. But if there is one new rule that you must learn, this is it: There are no old rules, only new ones.

What's difficult is working in the new world and being managed by others whose mind-sets are of the old. What worked for them ten years, five years, or even a few months ago is not necessarily best for you in your current job, facing your current problems.

Invest in yourself.

Make yourself adaptive, resilient, and valuable by learning what will work in many places, under many circumstances. Learn the six Pathways here and put them to use. Don't invest your future, your income, your family, and your sanity in anything less.

Go for results.

Don't go for effort that's just effort or for appearances or for acceptance. Go for tangible results you can point to and get credit for. It's unfortunate, but many total jerks get promoted or at least tolerated in business because they get results (sales, profitability, growth, clients, accounts, and the like). Results shield you from the attacks of competitors and strike fear into the hearts of those who entertain the thought of replacing you. You can always take your results elsewhere.

Know-what before know-how.

All the know-how in the world is useless unless it's the right know-how. *Knowing what* means using the appropriate technique at the appropriate time for the right reasons. In times of change, you can't assume the "what." Start thinking about the *whats* to do before the *hows* of doing them. Start thinking about what to avoid, what pays off, what's important, and what you're up against.

Get quick.

Good is okay, fast is better, but quick is best. Quick is a combination of speed and agility, the knack of moving fast and changing fast to move in another direction. Good basketball players shift from offense to defense as soon as a missed shot hits the rim; they're quick. Learn of upcoming trends, biases, and changes before everyone else and respond quicker. We're all in a competitive race, but the finish line is shifting from front to rear, side to side—instantaneously. Know how to detect this, how to pivot, and how to run fast in the new direction.

What Do I Do?

These rules are important, but they're difficult to act on. You need more specific tips to carry them out. You need direct, easy, and fast techniques that embody the new rules and bring immediate results. They need to be second nature for you, hard-wired into your thoughts and actions.

In the chapters that follow, you'll learn these techniques. You will start to see the new world of work as it really is, understand what separates the winners from the losers, and embark on a permanent program of advancement. As you put the techniques to use, you'll increase your own value, your durability, and your agility. You'll learn to not only survive and succeed but enjoy and master the challenges of change. And you'll end up doing what you like, and liking it.

The rewards will include increased income and increased impact on your surroundings: more dollars and more dents. Soon the survival techniques will become automatic, intuitive, second nature. Doors will open before you—doors to advancement, opportunity, and increased self-worth. How will this happen?

The Way It Works

I'll give you six powerful *Pathways* to excellence, each an express lane on the business highway. Each is designed to help on its own. But more commonly, you'll see how to progress from one to the other, through all six, in almost any work-related situation. Each Pathway is illustrated by Figure I-1 and briefly defined here.

1. *Break the sound barrier—the Listen Pathway.* Discovering ways to tune in to what's happening, what's needed, what works. Developing ways to "know what" in time to do something about it.

2. *Break the code to problems and opportunities—the Prospect Pathway.* Finding out what they hold and what you can do with them. Cutting through the confusion and getting to the heart of the issue quickly, easily. Not working hard, working smart.

3. *Break away from convention—the Innovate Pathway.* Getting what you want with what you have, often in simple ways but with stunning results. Getting beyond the thought barrier to break the rules and get ahead.

4. *Break the speed limit—the Respond Pathway.* Moving in new directions rapidly. Taking shortcuts to get to the payoff. Avoiding misspent effort and wasted time. Losers react to change, winners respond—lightning quick.

5. *Break into the future—the Adapt Pathway.* Reshaping yourself and your environment to better suit changed conditions. Fitting in easily with new demands, objectives, and circumstances. Learning to grow, improve, progress.

6. *Break out in front—the Lead Pathway.* Pulling others with you in the pursuit of excellence. Taking charge of

WELCOME TO CRUNCH TIME **15**

unconnected, uncontrolled events and making them work for you. Finding and using power vacuums. Becoming the type of leader the business world really needs.

Taking the Pathways

For each Pathway I'll give you five solid techniques for implementing it and describe five common barriers that might

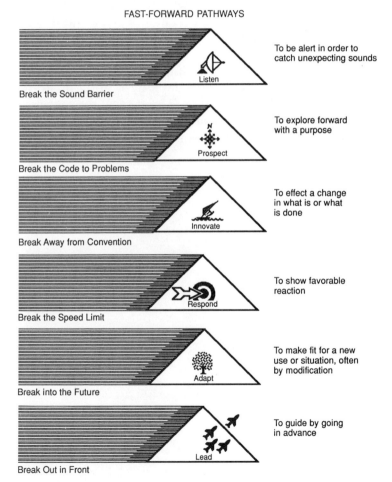

FAST-FORWARD PATHWAYS

Listen — To be alert in order to catch unexpecting sounds
Break the Sound Barrier

Prospect — To explore forward with a purpose
Break the Code to Problems

Innovate — To effect a change in what is or what is done
Break Away from Convention

Respond — To show favorable reaction
Break the Speed Limit

Adapt — To make fit for a new use or situation, often by modification
Break into the Future

Lead — To guide by going in advance
Break Out in Front

Figure I-1

keep you from choosing it. You'll learn when to apply each technique and what to expect when you do. And you'll see how each Pathway supports the others, how they connect and combine in a practical program. Each Pathway is enhanced with pictograms illustrating dos and don'ts, and you'll be given real-life examples of actual people, companies, products, and services that have taken these Pathways to sudden and sustained excellence.

In short, you have an organized, exciting journey ahead. The emphasis is on brevity, speed, and progress. Each Pathway and each technique is designed for rapid deployment, for quick jumps to higher levels of achievement and security. And each is designed to help you understand today's turbulent environment, implement today's most appropriate responses to it, and lift you above and away from the confusion and uncertainty that affects others—to help you move *fast-forward*. The journey is well worth it, for the self you save may be your own.

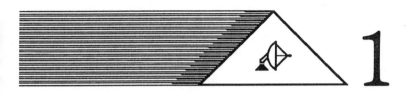

Break
the Sound Barrier

*There is no special talent required to listen
for change and appreciate its presence. All
we need is an attentive attitude, broad
interests, and a few practiced skills.*

The *Listen* Pathway

Learning to Breathe Again

Information is the oxygen of today. We need it to survive
and to grow. And, like oxygen, information surrounds us.
Learning to listen in changing times is no less vital than
learning to breathe. And it is no more difficult.

The stuff of survival, information is everywhere. It comes
from all directions, is relentless and at times overpowering. It
pours through computer screens, faxes, telephones, videos,
voice mail, newspapers, magazines, speeches, meetings, television, radios, and occasionally, real human beings. Some say

we are drowning in information. I say we drown when we stop breathing, when we stop taking it in.

Listening is the first of the six Pathways to survival and success. It represents the starting point for all the others. I use it as a metaphor for the receipt of information; whether it comes in the form of sound or not is unimportant. If you take it in from outside, you're listening. What it means, how it's used, and where it leads are all questions for the remaining Pathways. You can't get to them unless you have the raw material of knowledge, information, in all its richness and variety. And you can't get that unless you're listening better than you have been. This chapter will teach you why it's important to listen, how to listen better, and what to expect once you start breathing this "oxygen." You'll start to come alive, get smarter, and become stronger—all because you'll know how to listen again.

Quit Thinking and Start Listening _____

Listening is automatic at birth. But almost from the start, we develop habits or prejudices that limit our ability to receive the wealth of information that swirls around us. Because information announces threats as well as opportunities, we must work at listening. We must recognize its importance, remove its barriers, and keep ourselves constantly open to messages when they arrive. *To listen is to be alert in order to catch all unexpected sounds.*

Survival skills honed over thousands of years taught us to make quick decisions, speedy analyses, and on-the-spot judgments: friend or foe? good or bad? run or fight? now or later? But a rush to analyze or judge incoming information severely limits learning. To survive in change, *quantity* must be the goal. You'll want to receive as much meaning as possible from events and signals around you, and to do this you've got to postpone contemplating or studying them. Good listeners "let it all in" and sort it all out later. Most of all, good listeners seek out more and more sources, and different ones. They cast a wide net out into the world and receive as much information as possible. Sorting, analyzing, and acting on what we hear is left to the remaining Pathways. Listening has got to come first.

Are You a Good Listener?

Good listeners do ignore some messages. They ignore the rules of listening that no longer work. I'll list these for you here and let you decide if you believe any of them anymore. Read this list and see if you agree with any or all of the "lessons" of the past.

The Wrong Rules

1. You've got to concentrate to listen.
2. Shut out all distractions.
3. Pay attention to the key points.
4. Focus on those who know what they're talking about.
5. Learn everything you can about your occupation.

If you agree with any of these, it's time to rethink what listening is all about. Because these are just a few of the many misconceptions that might be holding you back. In times of turmoil, following these rules makes about as much sense as putting a plastic trash bag over your head and trying to walk across the San Diego freeway. If you're still following these rules, I hope to change your mind and to increase your chances of *saving yourself*. You'll find that listening the right way is easy. Listening the old way, the wrong way, is harder and more dangerous.

In place of the wrong rules listed above, I want you to consider their opposites. I want you to *break the rules* of listening you've been taught and start practicing the right rules, the ones that are better fitted to a world in change.

The Right Rules

1. Concentrate less and listen more.

2. Distractions: they can be important messages.

3. Pay attention to the incidental points.

4. Listen to those who might not know what they're talking about.

5. Learn about what's beyond the limits of your occupation.

Apprehending the World

I use *listening* as a term for apprehending the world, the changing, swirling, and unpredictable context in which we all live and work. It's a better metaphor than *seeing*, because to see you've got to look, to direct your attention at something and concentrate on it. Ears work whether we want them to or not. We listen even in our sleep. It's a nondiscriminating activity. We might decide where to look and what to see, but we don't do the same when we listen. We get the noise whether we want it or not, whether it was planned or unplanned. And because of this, we get a hell of a lot more information than if we had to seek it out and focus on it. It comes to us easily and freely. Once we get it, we can quickly decide whether it's waste or wisdom.

Asleep at the Wheel

Large corporations and entire industries have concentrated so well on what they do that they've forgotten to listen. When Japanese cars started showing up on the shores of California in the early seventies, Detroit's big three automakers took scant notice. They looked at the product and called it cheap. They looked at the size and called it small. They looked at the engines and called them puny. Then they looked at the 3 percent market share and called it insignificant. They knew what the imports were but didn't know what they meant. They didn't listen to the market. They ignored the customers buying these cars from overseas—never listened to them. They focused on their own products, concentrated on their own customers, stuck to the knitting, and fell asleep. When they woke up, it was too late. They had been looking inward but not listening outward for too long. They never heard Mr. Joe as he crept across the canvas. They didn't notice the crowd hush as he drew back his fist and aimed. I think that upon being promoted to vice president, each executive must have been issued a corner office, an administrative assistant, and a plastic trash bag.

The Secret of X-Rated Movies

Detroit wasn't the only city where business managers wore bags over their heads. In Hollywood, the "legitimate" film industry was excruciatingly slow in responding to the videocassette market. An outsider, an entrepreneur named Stuart Karl went from nowhere to production kingpin by listening to the message of pornographic videos. It seems these came out on video quickly, as soon as the VCR technology was here. Karl wondered why regular movies weren't coming out on video. "Nobody wants to see a movie more than once or twice, unless it's porno, so they won't buy them," he was told. That was conventional film wisdom. Karl wondered what people would watch over and over and over again...besides pornography. He thought of exercise videos, contacted Jane Fonda, and proceeded to make and sell the most popular film in the history of the medium, "Jane Fonda's Workout," and an unending string of sequels.

Getting to the Payoff

You don't have to be an entrepreneur or an executive to need listening. You need it to determine where you stand, where your company is headed, what jobs are hot and which ones are dead ends, and when and where to make your moves when turmoil starts brewing.

I'm going to tell you where to go to listen, how to soak in as much information as you can, how to uncover unexpected sources that might surprise you. You'll then learn how to get from the relatively passive action of listening to real results—how to leap from this Pathway to the others, where listening really pays off.

Fast-Forward Listening

The beauty of good listening is that it requires less effort, is more interesting, and yet is more powerful than bad listening. It's a strain to listen badly, but most of us do. It's a joy to listen well, and most of us should. Here are five key techniques to make you a better listener and establish yourself securely in this first Pathway.

1. *Ignore the main message.*   Secondary information is often more revealing than more direct types. Concentrating on the main message can shut out subtle, yet more valuable signals that are trying to reach us.

2. *Change your position.*   If we move in different circles, talk to different people, read different books, and expose ourselves to fresh experiences, we get new perspectives and sometimes powerful ideas.

3. *Don't judge or analyze.*   Judging and analyzing divert attention from other messages and act as filters, blocking out or distorting what information we do get.

4. *Listen to pain.*   Pain is a metaphor for bad news. But bad news (criticism, objections, and so on) tells us a lot. Sometimes it's priceless.

5. *Ask the amateurs.*   The experts don't have all the knowledge. Signals from customers, clients, and outsiders are often much more important.

Ignore the Main Message _____

Every company, every institution, and every organization has a "main message." It's the theme song, the anthem, the slogan that's repeated over and over, loud and strong. It might be a marketing pitch, like Ford Motor's "Quality is job one" or Coca-Cola's "It's the real thing." Or it might be a tired expression uttered by your boss, like "My door is always open," or "People are our most precious resource." Whatever, it keeps you from listening to more important, more subtle, and more meaningful messages.

The main message is like a command from Big Brother in the novel *1984*. It blasts into your consciousness and makes you numb. You start to believe it and take it for granted. You stop looking or listening for other alternatives, other conditions, other messages. My advice is to ignore it for a few days and see what it feels like to breathe pure oxygen, information that hasn't been contrived for consumption—real stuff.

Start by turning the main message around. You do this by thinking just the opposite of what it tells you to think. For example, how can Coke be the real thing when it's unnaturally made, has artificial colors and additives, and is pumped full of carbon dioxide? If that's real, I don't want to think about what an "unreal thing" could do to my system.

Every time your boss repeats, "My door is always open," ask yourself what she's trying to hide. When Wendy's hamburgers are touted as plump and juicy, could they be trying to cover up the fact that they're fatty and greasy? And when an executive starts saying people are his most valuable resource, it may be time to begin thinking that he's compensating for an impending layoff.

The Big Lie.   It's been called the *Big Lie*. And it often means that the opposite is true. When Eastern Airlines said, "We earn our wings every day," they had been consistently rated lowest in service by frequent fliers. When a theme is emphasized, it often means the company, product, or person giving the emphasis is really weak in that area. Otherwise they'd leave it alone. When a supervisor keeps telling me the door is always open, I begin to wonder if anybody ever visits that supervisor.

Likewise, when you think that quality is paramount in your outfit, you're not staying open to signals that it's not. You're hearing quality lectures, seeing quality films, and reading quality reports. You're not listening to nonquality lectures, seeing "here's-what's-shoddy" films, or reading "goof-up reports." Don't believe the Big Lie. It blocks out the Big Truth.

If you're a sales rep and you're told your customers are upwardly mobile, educated urban dwellers, you could be ignoring the rest of the world. If you're a productivity consultant, you could rightly say, "Ninety-five percent of my clients want increased productivity." No kidding. That's why they're your clients. But the guy across town could be selling ten times the amount of work in leadership training. You only hear people wanting productivity. You've become trapped by the main message.

There is no main message. There are thousands of important messages, and what's important to you today may not be so important tomorrow. Keep open to alternatives, keep listening for signals of change. Don't let one or even a few messages block out the rest. They could be the ones you desperately need to hear.

Change Your Position

Go somewhere different, meet different people, listen to things you don't like or don't care about, read magazines about things you hate, and breathe it all in. What you pick up at the sushi bar could be more important than what you pick up at a club meeting where everyone is like you: thinks the same, talks the same talk, and walks the same walk. Get away for a change.

Every commercial flight is full of business people. They're like clones, dressing almost identically, talking about the same things, and reading the same magazines. Instead of

Business Week or *Fortune*, they need to be reading *People,
Time, Datamation, Modern Maturity, Ebony, Triathlete,* or
Ducks Unlimited—anything that has absolutely nothing to do
with their sphere of work or interests. That's where ideas
come from. That's where something fresh, unexpected, and
sometimes vital is hiding. Let it reach you. It costs nothing. It
could be priceless.

**Attack of the Fortune-Telling, Bible-Thumping, Ginzu
Shrinks.** I've given hundreds of speeches and used to think
the way to improve was to give more speeches and to keep
practicing. I don't think that's true anymore. Now I scan the
cable TV offerings and get some of the best tips from watching wild preachers, Ginzu knife pitchmen, pop psychologists,
and fortune-tellers. I don't care about the impending apoca-
lypse, how to come to grips with sibling rivalry, or whether I
can slice a tomato after cutting a steel bar apart with the same
knife! I ignore the main message and let their styles teach
me. I try to learn from their tone of voice, gestures, pacing,
props, and expressions. I'm not going to be a better speaker
by speaking more. I'm learning by being spoken to. It's easier
and more effective. I change my position.

What They Might Not Want You to Know. One of my first
jobs after getting out of the Army was as a seismic analyst for
the Tennessee Valley Authority. I studied earthquakes and
used computer simulation programs to see how they might
affect the many nuclear power plants the Authority was con-
structing. It was dry, dull, dead-end work. I was attending
graduate school in business at night and had just gotten my
master's degree. Anxious for work on the business side and
bored to death by number crunching, I kept hearing how
TVA promoted and transferred from within. I applied for
several jobs in contract administration, hoping to get involved with vendors, builders, and outside consultants as a
TVA contract administrator. Months passed. No response
ever came from my applications...more number crunching.

One lunch break I happened to be reading a copy of the *Chicago Tribune* sent by a buddy's mother from back home. She sent it to him for the sports pages, but I started reading the want ads. There it was, a quarter-page ad looking for construction contract administrators—just apply to TVA! What? Here I was begging for the job and they were advertising in distant cities—and I had heard nothing! The position listed a phone number, which was four digits off my own work phone. It turned out the job was not only in my division, in my building, but on the same floor! I walked eighty feet from my desk and got the job—that day.

Take This Job and Post It.   It's a shame a guy in Knoxville, Tennessee, has to read the *Chicago Tribune* to find information about an attractive transfer to a department down the hall. But I did. I changed my listening position and my working position, and it paid off. Six months later I got a call from a headhunter. Contract administrators were in short supply, the power business was booming, and a large, international engineering firm needed them. I took off like a shot. Goodbye TVA! I'm taking my six months of experience and hitting the road!

A postscript: My father chastised me for leaving a "secure government job." Ten years later I read in the *New York Times* that TVA was laying off more than half its engineering work force. People with 10 to 15 years of experience were pushed out. So much for security. Thank God for the *Chicago Tribune*.

Don't Judge or Analyze

The only people who don't analyze or judge information as soon as they get it are the very stupid and the very smart. The very stupid don't know and don't care by nature. The very smart don't know and don't care by choice. They know that as soon as you start to analyze or judge, you stop listening. You filter, taint, or screen the rest of the message. You run the risk of missing something. *Quantity and diversity are the goals of good listeners*. Picking through the messages comes later. Don't try to sort it out until you've got it all.

If listening were a game of draw poker and our first two cards were a deuce and a nine, we'd fold right away. But the next three could be aces. Smart players wait until all five cards are dealt before they pick up their hands and start calculating their chances. But many of us act as if we're playing on *Jeopardy* and the clock is ticking. We can't wait to press the buzzer and blurt out our guess. Have you ever seen this show and noticed how often a contestant will jump on the buzzer before the question is complete and answer what he or she *thinks* the question is, only to get it wrong?

No one can afford to ponder everything, and accelerating change puts a premium on quick action. But if you want to *save yourself*, you've got to think clearly, feel deeply, and act wisely. And that means you've got to listen before you can prospect and innovate (the next two Pathways). This might take 30 days or 30 seconds depending on the situation, but it needs to take place in that sequence.

The Electronic Park Bench.   One warm, spring day a financial planner walked from her office tower in Los Angeles to a nearby restaurant for lunch. While her companions were discussing work, she was window-shopping along the way. One store they passed was a brokerage house, and she saw about a dozen senior citizens sitting in the waiting room watching a stock ticker with great interest. "Look at all those old people in there," she told her friend, who quipped, "Looks like the brokerage firm is taking the place of the park bench for old folks with nothing to do with their time." Another added, "I'm sure it's more comfortable for them, and besides, the pigeons don't bother them."

Everybody laughed, except the financial planner. She was too busy "listening." Months later she established an investment club for senior citizens and enrolled over 200 accounts. She'd done some research and discovered the wealth being invested by retired people and that they like to give their business to those who treat them with special care. She didn't have to come up with the idea as quickly as her companions came up with their flip remarks. She just took it in and thought about it later. They lost, she won.

Listen to Pain

If everything that was good for us caused pleasure and everything that hurt us caused pain, the average life span of a human being would be about 150 years. Octogenarians would be pole-vaulting in the Olympics. The problem is that many actions that harm us cause pleasure, and what's good for us often brings pain.

Why else would people smoke, drink to excess, take drugs, overeat, drive at excessive speeds, or otherwise endanger themselves? These bring pleasure. Why else do people avoid exercise and trips to the dentist? These cause pain. Pain tells us to quit doing what we're doing. But people throughout the business world are not listening to telling pain, to messages that say, "Something is wrong here." They're stumbling along blissfully toward a cliff, all the way singing, "Everything Is Beautiful." Thank God for pain. It keeps us from doing what's stupid, wrong, or dangerous. We need to seek it out and pay attention to it.

How Your Grandfather Became Your Grandfather. The nervous system is built around pain. And the role of pain is programmed into evolution. If your grandfather didn't have a nervous system that felt pain, he'd probably have sat on the potbelly stove to get warm. Then after about ten minutes of this, he'd sniff the air and say, "Hey, Mabel, are you cooking bacon?"

We don't have a nervous system that makes us change what we're doing on the job, that tells us we've got the wrong job or alerts us to impending change. We still need to listen to pain, but we've got to seek it out first. It usually doesn't come directly, if it comes at all, until it's too late.

No Pain, No Brain.   Except in rare cases, people whom we've offended, turned off, or failed to impress don't tell us. They just leave us alone. Customers don't complain if your company isn't attractive. They just don't become your customers, and you never hear from them. You get the damage but not the pain. When the restaurant serves mediocre, overpriced food, few people storm into the kitchen and complain. They just don't return. Then the manager struts around a half-empty dining room and says to himself, "We must be doing pretty good. No one's complaining." No pain, no brain.

It takes time and effort to complain, and most people would rather not bother. Why should they spend their energy telling you what you're doing wrong? They'd just as soon go across the street and try another place. When alternatives multiply and competition is intense, people simply move on. They don't have to straighten you out.

Almost every hotel says it's listening to its customers. They all set little "How are we doing?" cards in each room. I'm sure they're on the right track, that they get a lot of valuable information from the few of these they receive. But when I absolutely hate a hotel, I don't miss my plane out of town by filling out a form for them. If they really wanted to know, they'd make a form saying, "Tell us how bad we really are."

When you want to know how bad you're doing, ask. Ask directly. Don't expect your boss, your customers, or your peers to be following you around with a clipboard, ticking off your grades. Look for pain and listen to it when you find it.

Mixing Management With Margueritas.   At one time I designed a seminar on project management for Arthur Andersen & Co.'s Management Information Consulting Division, which is an international consulting firm in its own right—the largest on earth. Two of their partners and I were in a bar in Mexico City after having taught the three-day session at the University of Mexico. As an experiment, I had developed an hour-long topic on contract management, and we had given it as part of the final day's program. Over drinks we discussed the results.

The senior partner asked the junior one for his view. "I don't think we should keep that topic," he replied. "It caused the most confusion, confrontation, and debate. Everybody was interrupting, arguing, even screaming. It was chaotic!" As I sat silently, the senior partner considered this remark carefully. I was worried that he'd cancel the topic and my experiment would fail. But he turned to me and said, "Can you expand this topic into a separate three-day seminar? Obviously a lot of companies are struggling with contract management and need help." I agreed. The guy was listening to pain. We went on to give the new seminar over fifty times throughout Europe, Asia, Africa, and North America. The initial presentation was overbooked, and we had to hold three overflow sessions back-to-back. It was a big hit, one of the most successful, most popular training programs Arthur Andersen & Co. has ever produced. If what you try causes people to think differently, elevates their adrenaline level or blood pressure, you might be onto something. If it causes none of these reactions, it's probably a dud.

Ask the Amateurs

Oftentimes the ones with the least knowledge of a subject have the most essential information and the clearest insight into it. These are the amateurs, the ones who have no vested interest in the outcome, no ax to grind, no personal theory to prove. Listen to them. They can come up with pure gold.

Every expert has an invisible partner. It's the voice of reason, rationale, and restraint inside him or her. It's the voice that says, "Naaaa...I'd better not say that," or "Naaa...I might look stupid if I...." Experts are paid in dollars or respect for getting things right, for having the correct answer and for having it quickly, without much hesitation or qualification. For that reason they typically play it safe. Don't expect them to suggest the unusual, atypical, or risky. They've got a lot at stake in their recommendations. They won't or can't give you candor, spontaneity, or something that's so far off-the-wall it's right on target.

What Experts and Drunks Have in Common. Experts are also trained to think in certain structured ways, and this can limit their insight. You may have heard the story of the man who left a bar late at night and lost his car keys on the way to the parking lot. A passerby found him looking in the street under a lamppost and asked why he was looking in that particular spot. "Because this is where the light is," he replied. Experts tend to look where the light is, along the grain of their training, within their special field, or in the direction of their biases. The answers can be elsewhere. You may learn more from the naive, the unaffected, and the innocent. Listen to them.

Guess Who the Japanese Listen To. One of the most touted Japanese management techniques is their *Kanban* system, also known as just-in-time or JIT. It's where they order parts for a manufacturing line only when they're needed and don't waste money and space with incoming material inventory and storage. It's like ordering a Domino's pizza. You pick up the phone, call a supplier, and 30 minutes later a truck loaded with steel shows up at your receiving dock. Kanban and JIT experts are springing up everywhere. There are JIT systems, seminars, books—you name it.

I was touring a Japanese automaker's plant in Kawasaki one day and listening to the Japanese engineers rave about how great they were, how they invented JIT. That night I asked about it again over dinner. My Japanese host told me he'd learned it at the university, but he really knew what it meant by listening to a construction worker in the States. He was attending a convention in Manhattan, happened to walk by a construction site, and noticed the absence of building materials on the ground. "How come no construction material and equipment nearby, for quick use?" he asked an ironworker. "Can't afford it," he was told. "If we leave anything sitting for a few hours, it gets stolen or spray painted. We wouldn't have any place to put it anyway. We just call, and it comes when we want it." So much for the Japanese invention of JIT. Ask the amateurs.

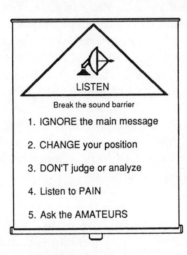

Barriers to Breaking the Sound Barrier

Sometimes it's difficult to become a better listener because so much works against you. Whether they are intentionally erected or not, barriers to listening can be found in your organization's culture, its external environment, or even deep within you. Recognizing and removing these barriers is the first step toward *saving yourself*. We all recognize habit, carelessness, and lack of concern as common barriers to effective listening. But there are others. You can't improve listening with a slogan, an order, or a training program. You've got to find and destroy the barriers. You've got to continually practice the skills and stay constantly alert to new threats to good listening. Here are the most common ones.

1. Success. This is the world champion. Success lulls us into a false sense of superiority. You've heard it said many times, "We're so good, others can learn from us." Any time a person or a company feels it has achieved the ultimate, it shuts out alternatives and other perspectives. It stops being hungry for information, and it stops considering ways to improve. If there is one rule of excellence, it's this: You can't stand still. Nobody owns success. You just lease it for a while. And you renew your lease daily by listening and learning, and then changing.

2. Dedication to One Answer. No matter how good it is, there is always a better way to do something. If we think we've got *the* answer, or the *only* answer, we stop listening. There is nothing wrong with being dedicated to our jobs or our goals, but our methods can always be improved. We won't know how or how much unless we admit that better ways are possible.

3. Rush to Judgment. Human nature works against us here. We jump to conclusions or make premature assessments before all the data are in. Judgment is a filter closing off the rest of the incoming information. The time to draw the picture is when most of the dots are on the page. Wait.

4. Premature Action. A bias toward action can be dangerous as well as beneficial. We often start formulating a response before we've got enough information to make a sensible one. A balance is needed between "paralysis by analysis" and "fools rush in."

5. Living in a Rut. Tune into all frequencies, not just one or two. Widen your listening by exposing yourself to new sources, new positions, and fresh perspectives. Answers and ideas come from all directions.

Do Something Different

Listening means being open and exposed, conditions most
business books tell you to avoid. This is sheer nonsense. The
risk isn't that we expose ourselves to criticism by listening, it's
that we expose ourselves to harm if we don't. Being exposed
means getting out from under that protective barrier of
sameness that surrounds most of us, that fixed position,
habit, or niche. *I want you to take active steps to do this.* I suggest you try it for a week and see if it gives you the tremendous payback I've seen in other cases.

Here's a list of recommendations. During the next week,
do at least one of the following, if not all of them.

1. *Read a magazine that you would never buy, thoroughly.*
Look carefully at the advertisements and imagine the audi-
ence these companies are trying to reach. List the three top
concerns of a typical reader, from what you can gather. See
why they're different from yours. Hear what they're telling
you.

2. *Eat in a different restaurant.*   Not just another version
of what you prefer but a completely new type. If you frequent Japanese and Chinese, go Mexican. If you dine conti-
nental or on seafood, sit through lunch at a deli. Take note
of the food, menu, customers, staff, decorations, conversa-
tions, and mood.

3. *Change your schedule.*   If you shop for food at night,
go in the morning. If you drive your car, take the bus. If you
go out for lunch, stay in. If you arrive at work at 8:30 a.m.,
come in at 7:30. Do this just once. See what you hear.

4. *Change the channel.*   If you watch the "CBS Evening
News," watch NBC or CNN. If you listen to rock music in
your car, tune into country & western. If you attend pro basketball games, go to a boxing match. Are the people different? Are their concerns different? Are the ideas and answers
different?

5. *Sit through an entire meeting without talking, as much as is polite.* Don't feel you have to lead it, add to it, or respond to other people's suggestions. Soak it all in. Notice the order in which people speak. Note their body language, their expressions, their intensity. If you must participate, do so at the very end. You'll be surprised how much more attention you get. And how much more you learn.

6. *Go to a meeting you don't need.* If you're working in marketing, ask if you can attend an R&D product meeting. If you're in accounting, go to a sales meeting. If you're in manufacturing, go to a meeting of purchasing agents. Just listen. How many of their problems are yours? How do they approach problems and opportunities? How do they see themselves?

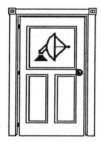

1. SUCCESS

2. DEDICATION to one answer

3. RUSH to judgment

4. PREMATURE response

5. Living in a RUT

Using the Listen Pathway

Listening is the ticket you buy to enter the other Pathways. It starts when you imagine yourself as a movable antenna, like a satellite dish that can swivel 360 degrees and constantly shift to new locations. Keep quantity, not quality, as your goal. Resist the impulses to judge, analyze, and respond to what you receive; that's for later. Keep telling yourself that you don't have to do anything with the information, just take it all in. Admit that you will never know all there is to know about anything and that you can never stop listening, even when you're deep into the Pathways that follow.

Then What?

I started this chapter by calling information the oxygen of our time and saying that listening is as easy and vital as breathing. No one can survive without breathing, but breathing alone doesn't qualify you to save yourself. It only lets you live. More skills are needed, but none can be gained unless you're first alive.

As you sharpen your listening ability, you'll move into the sorting, analyzing, and thinking modes. You'll be able to glean important messages and instructions for personal development and advancement. The stuff of success will be all around you.

PictoGame—Round 1

As a way of wrapping up your understanding of the Listen Pathway, I've devised some simple pictograms for you to consider. On the following page, you'll see five of these, each depicting a violation of one or more principles contained in this chapter. I'd like you to look them over and see if you can identify which barrier to listening (or which technique) they depict. Don't worry about whether you get the same answer as I did, just try to have some fun with them. They might help you visualize listening a bit better and stimulate your thinking about ways in which it can be improved. You'll find the answers I chose in the PictoGame Answer section at the back of the book.

WHAT'S WRONG WITH THESE PICTURES?

1. _____

2. _____

3. _____

(Continued)

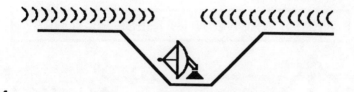

4. _____

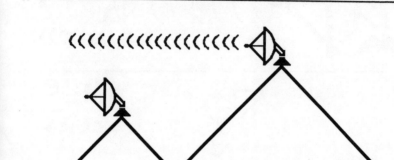

5. _____

Break the Code
to Problems

*The only way to fail at Prospecting is to
avoid it.*

The *Prospect* Pathway

Finding Patterns Behind the
Confusion

If following the Listening Pathway is like strip mining, scooping in all the available information in massive quantities, the
next step is to search through what you've picked up. I call it
prospecting, a metaphor for exploring forward with a purpose. Our purpose is to find relationships, to refine raw information into meaning. Then we can move quickly to the
other Pathways, especially Innovation and Response.

Psychologists tell us that the most severe forms of mental
retardation are evidenced by a failure to find patterns, the
inability to see how things and ideas link up. On the other
hand, some of the world's greatest geniuses were able to

make connections, to see patterns where no one else could. Who but Einstein would have seen the connection between energy and mass? Who but Louis Pasteur saw the connection between bacteria and infection? Everyone else looked at genes and saw a scrambled mess of acids. It took Watson and Crick to see the simplicity and elegance of the double helix in DNA: the very pattern of life.

Pulling Secrets Out of the Swirl

These great thinkers teased patterns out of chaos. They discovered connections and hidden links in what other people saw as confusion. Since we live in times of turmoil, of rapid change and even chaos, the patterns that do present themselves often change quickly. The prospecting techniques in this chapter won't necessarily lead to world-shattering discoveries, but they will help you see patterns of threats and opportunities. They will help you make sense out of what's happening or about to happen...in time to do something about it. When relationships and rules are being rearranged, the person who can detect the new patterns first usually wins. I call these the *prospectors*, those singular individuals who have the courage, the insight, and the skills to find meaning where others see mystery, to detect patterns where others see a mess—in other words, to pull secrets of success from the swirl of daily events.

If you master the skill of prospecting, you'll find answers to pesky problems before others do, see reasons behind baffling events, and open new doors to understanding. These abilities are no longer optional, they're vital. For as the world in which we work changes more and more rapidly, and more unpredictably, the ones who can make sense of things quickly are the only ones who will survive and move ahead.

Finding Problems, Solving Opportunities

Others will tell you the way to get ahead is to *solve problems* and *find opportunities*. These skills worked well in the stable past and are still key. But today's winners turn this advice inside out. They *find problems* and *solve opportunities*.

Before you can mine a vein of opportunity, you've got to prospect for it—to "explore forward with a purpose." The purpose of prospecting is to look for connections, to find and trace problems back through their symptoms to their sources, and to find and solve hidden opportunities overlooked by others. Prospectors are viewed by others as different, and indeed they are. They are fearless in where they go and what they ask. They're trying to connect the dots of data around them and make pictures. Like good listeners, prospectors aren't judgmental or choosy, they're just inquisitive. And they don't get sidetracked or waylaid as they pursue the objects of their dedication: survival and success.

Humans Do It!

To be human is to prospect: to find and solve puzzles. No one could survive past infancy without having some prospecting skills. Prospecting helps us understand the world and allows us to go about making it better. The only way to fail at prospecting is to avoid it, to assume the problems of today are the same as yesterday, or that the opportunities are so hidden and complex that someone else is better able to get to them. The truth is you can get to them, and you must. Otherwise you'll be stopped in your tracks, stuck back on the Listening Pathway. You'll hear a lot but know absolutely nothing.

The Prospecting Belief System

Business prospectors are confident, fearless, and driven. They'll go anywhere, ask anything, and consider everything in their quest to improve, to master today's challenges. They also have a strange belief system, one best illustrated by the following tenets. I'll list them here and then describe what each means in detail.

What Prospectors Believe

1. Sometimes things ARE exactly as they seem.

2. Problems and opportunities come in clusters.

3. Every answer is a partial answer.

4. Some people don't want answers or solutions.

5. *They* really *don't* know.

6. All that glitters is air.

7. Knowledge is ownership.

Nothing to Hide

If a prospector walked into a desert and immediately spotted a mountain of glittering gold, he wouldn't ask himself, "What's the gimmick here?" He'd fill his pockets and load his mule with as much as he could, then head for town a rich man. Problems and opportunities aren't always hiding or written in code. Sometimes they are exactly what they seem, no deciphering required.

Experimenters have placed purses and billfolds on busy sidewalks and filmed as hundreds of people pass them by. Most suspect that it's a trick or a game. We do the same in our work. We see conspiracies that aren't there, imagine motives that don't exist, suppose complexity where simplicity reigns. Go for the easy answer first. See if that's the real answer. Don't hold yourself back by the apparent simplicity of most problems and the apparent ease of most solutions. Sometimes things are exactly as they seem. They *look simple* and they *are simple*.

Like Snakes in a Basket

Problems and opportunities coexist everywhere. They're usually intertwined like snakes in a basket, and it's hard to tell one from the other. Toxic waste becomes a multibillion dollar industry. An influenza outbreak sends patients flocking to doctors, who are able to pay their mortgages and feed their families because of it. When peace breaks out, the military starts to worry. Rising interest rates thrill investors and chill new home buyers.

Whenever you see a problem, look for a benefit or an opportunity close by, in the same basket. Chances are you'll find one quickly. When changes occur, new problems spring up all around. That's why to win in changing times, you should practice problem *finding*. Find tomorrow's problems, and you'll get a handle on tomorrow's solutions.

Good News, Bad News

The converse is true too. Opportunities always create new problems. Miracle breakthroughs in biotechnology create ethical worries. Successful interdiction of cocaine from outside our borders creates demand for a new, more addictive domestic product: methamphetamine—ice. Well-insulated, energy-conserving homes trap dangerous radon gas in high concentrations. Lower gasoline prices encourage more travel by car. Result: more accidents, more pollution, less oil exploration, recession in our energy states.

There's the story of an international shoe company that sent a salesman to a remote African country. He wired back to the home office, "Bad news! No one here wears shoes." The home office wired back, "Good news. No one there wears shoes!"

Half Enough Is Good Enough

If you've got an idea that partially solves a problem or partially capitalizes on an opportunity, go for it! Problems that are fixed often stay fixed only for a while. So what? Your challenge is to move ahead, not to come up with the total, irrevocable, incontestable, final solution.

Band-Aids don't heal wounds or stop all cuts from becoming infected. But let a child get cut on the playground, and the first words out of the nearest adult are, "Better get a Band-Aid on that right away." Your idea might be a Band-Aid solution, but a bleeding patient won't argue with it.

Why Race a Bear?

The story of the two campers illustrates this point better. Inside their tent one dark night, they heard the unmistakable growl of an approaching bear. One guy peeked outside and quickly jerked his head back in screaming. "It's a bear all right!" he said as he started hurriedly putting on his sneakers. "Hey," his buddy remarked, still in his sleeping bag, "why would you need your sneakers? There's no way in the world you can outrun a full-grown bear."

"I don't have to outrun a full-grown bear," he responded. "I just have to outrun you!"

That's the story of competition. You only have to be a little bit better than the rest. Your idea might be full of holes, but if it's better than what's in place right now, it's the best it has to be. Don't strive for perfection. Strive for what works better than what exists. That's all you need. And in times of turmoil, that's the most anyone can expect. Besides, people who wait for perfection—and achieve it or something close to it—often get overlooked and belatedly labeled ahead of their times. Unfortunately, belated praise never helps you *save yourself*.

What About When They Don't Want It Fixed?

If a prospector hauled a load of gold into town and found that no one wanted it, that it was suddenly out of favor, he'd probably go looking for silver, topaz, or uranium. He surely wouldn't go back into the mountains and risk his life for more gold. When you find a solution or develop a great fix and no one wants it, move on to other challenges. There could be hidden reasons why no one wants the problem solved or wants to live with the solution.

Years ago a company making razor blades toyed with the idea of a permanent hair-removal cream. Just by wiping it on once, a man would never have to shave again. Wow! What a market, what a potential profit! Only trouble was that surveys said men would overwhelmingly reject the stuff. Seems men like the idea of having to shave. They don't want to give up the ability to grow facial hair forever. They'd rather spend every morning, in perpetuity, scraping, mowing, pulling, and otherwise ravaging their faces. They prefer the problem to the solution.

You probably haven't invented a permanent depilatory, but I'll bet you've come up with unwanted solutions. You come up with a suggestion that makes all the sense in the world, but if it eliminates someone's job, causes people to change, diminishes someone's authority, or requires a little extra work, it gets stonewalled. When this happens, don't spend any more energy trying to convince everyone that it's a good idea. Look into that basket of snakes and attack the problems that your solution creates. Fix them, and the solution will sail through. If it still doesn't, start looking for silver, topaz, or uranium. Move on. They don't want it to be fixed. You could be on a kamikaze mission.

They Really Don't Know

Quite often people really don't know what they should. Not knowing this, you might keep looking for a more complex answer. With the easy answer staring you in the face, you keep questioning your own intelligence and getting more frustrated. It's so simple, you tell yourself, everybody must know it. But don't be fooled. Many simple fixes only seem simple to you because you've come up with them. Don't be afraid to suggest the painfully obvious. Many times it's only obvious to you. They really *don't* know.

Ninety-Five Percent of What We Sell Is Air

While going to college, I worked nights in a convenience store. My boss owned the place and five others like it around town. He had a high school education and a net worth of several million dollars. One night as we were closing, he looked around the empty store pensively and told me, "You know, 95 percent of what we sell is air."

If he had to revise that statement today, he'd up the percentage to 99. Madonna was wrong. We live in an *immaterial* world. When you buy a box of breakfast cereal, take away the packaging, the promises of regularity, the assurance of fiber and no cholesterol, the image of a cozy, Sunday morning meal with the ones you love, and what do you get? A few ounces of smashed, dried corn seeds. The rest is simply "air." At least with a box of corn flakes you get something tangible. What do you get when you buy life insurance, pay taxes, or watch a movie? You get air. Virtually everything we buy and sell each other is nonmaterial. We buy designs, ideas, concepts, thoughts, images, impressions, permissions, assurances, and symbols. A complex, intricate European automobile can cost over one hundred thousand dollars, but put it in a crusher and you get a couple of cubic feet of matter. We buy the designer's ideas, the advertiser's promises, the dealer's real estate taxes, the currency exchange fees, safety and fuel consumption testing by the manufacturer, the export or import licenses for the components, the medical insurance for the workers who put the tires on, and the programmer's time for the software that runs the robotic painting machines. The material component is negligible.

Making Things With Thoughts

The book you are reading is another example. I've written it, but I've never seen it. I don't know where it was printed or bound. I don't know a thing about how it's made or sold, or where. Everything you get from the book is nonmaterial. All you have are my thoughts—air. You've a small rectangle of cardboard and paper with ink symbols less than a millimeter thick. The pages might be numbered, but what count are the ideas, not the paper.

It's always been true, but it's getting more so every day. *The thought content of every product is overtaking the material content.* Records, tapes, films, and books are examples. So are software, computer chips, psychological counseling, dental work, and legal advice. Thoughts are what turn a few grains of sand into a microprocessor and a pound of paper into a bible. They turn a fistful of smashed corn into a healthy heart and a cozy breakfast with your spouse.

I mention this trend only to emphasize the value of thoughts, of ideas, designs, and solutions you may come up with. Don't think you need a factory, a block of real estate, or money in the bank to succeed today. Most entrepreneurs start with nothing but thoughts. By the thousands they're capitalizing on their imaginations, know-how, and ideas. You can too. You can never overestimate the value of prospecting, of finding problems and solutions and connecting them. All that glitters is not gold. It's mostly air. Today's prospectors are going after air with a passion.

Knowledge Is Ownership

In the early days of navigation, European states punished by death anyone who stole a "rudder" or ship's map of the coastline. Knowledge of what reefs, shoals, and winds existed out there was that precious, a national resource, what we'd call "competitive advantage." And it used to be that someone thought they owned you when they had you captured and imprisoned behind stone walls. Now they own you when they *know* you, when they've gotten your "rudder," your knowledge of what and how work is accomplished.

This suggestion is a very self-serving or self-preserving one. Some would call it mercenary. I can just advise you to be a little mysterious, a little guarded with your knowledge. No prospector would fight much if you tried to steal his shovel or mule. But go for his maps and you're looking down the wrong end of a gun barrel. In today's information age, when knowledge is the greatest asset most of us possess, you should protect it as vigorously.

The Dark Side of Knowledge

Knowledge, connections between problems and solutions, is what fuels innovation. And innovation is the payoff for all the listening and prospecting you're learning to do. I'm not suggesting you keep everything you know under lock and key, or avoid discussions, suggestions, or training of others. I'm suggesting you get some of the benefit for what you know. And on the dark side, I've seen many people tossed out by companies who think they've gotten all their knowledge, thank you. I want you to drive past knowledge to action and results.

The Smart Hammer

Every consultant knows this, and everyone else should. The old story of the manufacturing guru tells it all. He was called to help reactivate a stalled production line. Material was spoiling, parts were backing up, and customer orders were going unfilled. He spent a few minutes examining the complex machinery, then took a hammer from a nearby worker and gave one piece a small rap. Bam! The line kicked in and started humming. Everything was back to normal. "That'll be one thousand dollars," he told his client.

"What? All you did was hit the machine! How can you charge a thousand dollars for that?"

"I'm not," the consultant replied. "I'm charging you 5 bucks for hitting the machine and 995 bucks for *knowing where* to hit it."

We're all like that consultant. We're paid for what we know and how we put that knowledge to use. Without knowledge or skill, we're an expense to most of our employers and a nuisance to our customers. How do we survive today? We increase our knowledge and skill, and we increase our ability to change it once conditions change. We learn, and we learn how to unlearn and learn again, quickly. We become good prospectors. Here are five ways to do it.

Fast-Forward Prospecting

1. *Look for little things.*   Most major problems are ultimately the result of minor causes. Smart prospectors check the valleys first, then head for the mountains. Never overlook the obvious, or the easy.

2. *Write the problem in one sentence.*   Problems and opportunities can get unnecessarily complex and confusing. This simple exercise forces us to reduce them to their essential elements, and it separates symptoms from causes rather quickly. Sometimes there are two or more problems combined, and uncoupling them is the first step to solving each one.

3. *Pretend it's fixed.*   Maybe the solution is unwanted. By pretending it's fixed, we often surface other, more critical problems. And it could be that we prefer to live with the initial one. Try it. It's easy, and it's free.

4. *Ask the crazy question.*   This is the one everyone else is afraid to ask, but should. Don't worry about appearing naive or foolish. Only those who never ask are naive or fool-

ish. Prospecting means not being overly concerned about the way the treasure is found, but about finding it.

5. *Understand the word* "can't." It's often used to mean "won't," "don't want to," "don't know how to," or "am afraid to." Keep asking until you're convinced that "we can't" really means "we can't." Otherwise, it means "we can if we try."

It's the Little Things That Count _____

One of the world's most popular appointment calendars is made by DAY-TIMERS, Inc. Customers buy a year's supply of notebook refills and keep track of their schedules, business expenses, and the like. The problem with selling new refills is that people put off ordering them until they're out. Then they spend a few weeks without a calendar, could buy a competitor's product, and leave the DAY-TIMERS' fold.

To solve this problem, DAY-TIMERS uses a simple solution. They embed an order form in each of the last few months' inserts. You can't avoid seeing it and considering re-ordering. When you open your calendar to make an entry, there's the renewal form. Simple. Easy. It works better than any reminder letters, advertising messages, or phone calls.

Here's the logic: People need to be reminded and the re-ordering needs to be easy, almost impulsive. People look at the calendar every day. Stick the form in the calendar. That's the link between problem and solution.

We've all read of a jetliner being brought down in midair because of the failure of a 19-cent screw. If a 19-cent screw can bring down an airliner, can't a 19-cent screw keep it flying? Simple solutions can be found inside complex problems.

Write the Problem in One Sentence _____

This helps pull the snakes apart. Then you can go after them one at a time. It's also a powerful tool for group discussions, consensus building, and brainstorming. Try this trick the next time your group discusses a thorny problem. Ask each person to write the entire problem in one short sentence, without collaboration. Then collect their slips of paper and read the results to the group, without identifying the originators. The results might shock you. In fact, you might wonder if you all work for the same company, speak the same language, or inhabit the same world.

To give you examples, I've taken some of today's most persistent problems, the ones that make headlines at least once a week, and written each in one sentence. See what you think:

1. The Arab-Israeli Conflict

"They think it's their country and we know it's ours."

It doesn't matter which side is making the statement, it's true for both. Another alternative is, "Two peoples, one land."

2. U.S. Airline Deregulation

"You can get out, but you can't get in."

Companies can go bankrupt, get gobbled up by competitors, or shrink to insignificance. But who can start up a major airline today? It takes too much time, money, and talent. The net result: fewer airlines, decreased competition.

3. The Decline of Daily Newspapers

"Watching is easier than reading."

Television is killing the papers. All across the nation they're folding like lawn chairs at the end of summer vacation. With so little time in each day and so many of us spending our work time with written words, TV is less demanding and therefore more popular. Newspapers know this. That's why *USA Today*'s sales racks are designed to look like television sets, the stories are shorter, and the pictures are in color.

4. The U.S. Trade Deficit

"We sell thoughts and buy things."

Trade figures reflect goods that cross borders. They don't capture the buying and selling of designs, patents, licenses, book rights, or consulting services, not to mention scores of other nonmaterial sales from the United States to others. Since the United States "exports" information on a scale much greater than any imports, we show a deficit. But according to some experts, if these nonmaterial exports were considered, we could be running a surplus. Other experts suggest we're not selling our "air" at a high enough price.

5. The Failure of the Communist Economic System

"When everyone owns it, no one takes care of it."

This is why people toss trash out of their cars and onto the roadside but wouldn't think of doing the same in their front yards. It's also why communal farms in the Soviet Union produce one-seventh of their equivalents in our farm belt, where farmers own their land.

Pretend It's Fixed

The secret to playing good pool is not just making a good shot but making it in a way that leaves you in good position for the *next* shot, and the one after that. If you've made an easy shot but leave the cue ball between the eight ball and the cushion, you've solved one problem and created a much more difficult one.

Good prospectors think about the next move. They know that many problems aren't solved because the solution is a greater problem. Or at least it seems greater. Think about the problems that won't go away. Then consider what their solutions will cost. When you're in a meeting and everyone seems to be challenging a proposal, play the "pretend it's fixed" game. See if everyone is prepared to live *without* the problem. You may uncover the real reason why the "fix" is resisted.

The Crazy Question ───────────────

The crazy question challenges you and others to go against the grain of conventional wisdom. It's the one that nobody expects, and it always causes a sudden pause in the discussion. It forces you to justify what most take for granted: the so-called unwritten rules. And it often leads to more intense consideration of what work you're doing, why you're doing it, and how else it might be done.

Understand the Word *Can't* ───────────────

You've heard it a hundred times: "We can't do that." I want you to push past this word. I want you to keep asking until you know what the word *can't* really means. My guess is that the "can't barrier" is about as strong as wet tissue paper. Restate their objection without using the word *can't*. When they say, "We can't do that," you should ask, "Does that mean you don't want to do it, don't know how to do it, are afraid to do it, or don't want it done?" See if the real snakes jump out of that basket. Then step on them, one by one.

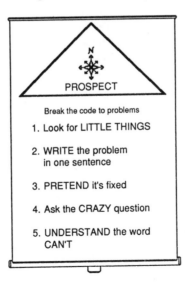

Barriers to Breaking the Code

Prospectors aren't afraid to get their boots muddy with problems. But sometimes the mud gets pretty deep. Or the territory that needs exploring is closed off to all but the most determined among us. And there usually aren't any maps to go by. In fact, that's the purpose of prospecting: to find the paths and to create the maps.

A common barrier comes from within: the feeling that it isn't our job...or that someone else takes care of these things. To survive and thrive, each organization needs as many prospectors as it can get. Finding problems and solving opportunities are everyone's job. We are all born inquisitive. What keeps us from exercising this talent?

1. Fear of the Unknown. Prospecting takes courage. Confronting the unknown has always been dangerous and unpredictable. There is no easy answer here, but as Hermann Hesse wrote, "Only the weak are sent on paths without perils."

2. A Closed Culture. A closed culture, corporate or otherwise, erects fences between itself and the rest of the world. The idea is that what's inside the fence is good and what's outside is bad. People from these cultures never venture outside. They don't say, "Stop the world, we want to get off"; they say, "We've gotten off, so stop the world." Some call it NIH, the "not invented here" syndrome. If we didn't invent it, it's no good.

Nothing could be more stupid. A closed culture sees the world beyond its borders as *terra incognita*—unknown territory. And as with the ancient maps, terra incognita marks the boundaries of safety and the beginning of the new world. The fear was that horrifying monsters dwelt there. But the truth was, that's where the gold and silver were to be found.

3. The Fast Answer. Some people would rather have a fast answer than a good one. They look for blame or excuses rather than solutions. And they rejoice when they find the "easy no," a quick reason to continue what they're doing and reject any alternatives. The world is full of easy noes. Anyone can find them. Would a prospector quit after the first shovel turns up "no gold"? "No" is the fastest answer to anything.

4. The Total Answer.   This is another reason to quit prospecting: finding the answer to everything. We know it as an excuse—declaring victory and pulling out. When you hear the words "the only way," you are hearing the end of improvement. And when you stop improving, you stop saving yourself.

5. Expecting the Complex.   This keeps many folks from even starting out as prospectors. They think it takes a degree in rocket science or that the solution must be so complex that someone would have found it before. Or when a simple solution is suggested, they dismiss or ridicule it. Simplicity isn't the same as stupidity. It could represent brilliance.

1. FEAR of the unknown

2. A CLOSED culture

3. The FAST Answer

4. The TOTAL Answer

5. Expecting the COMPLEX

Look for the Green

If you've ever been around small children, this has happened to you. While you're trying to explain something to them, like how to tie their shoes, they come up with an unexpected, expansive question that knocks you off your feet—like "Why is the sky blue?" or "Why are some people rich and others

poor?" or "Why is it okay to kill enemy soldiers but not someone who's mean to you?" Most of us revert to the old standby,
"Ask your father (or mother)."

I used to pester the devil out of my father with these questions. One day he told me to ask my mother. I said she told
me to ask him. He cursed a few times, thought a while, then
told me he was going to stop this incessant questioning once
and for all. He was going to give me one answer that would
work for virtually every question I'd ever have in life. I wig-
gled in anticipation. Wow! As a rookie prospector, I was
about to be introduced to King Solomon's mine!

My father pulled out his billfold and slowly retrieved a dollar bill. He waved it in my face and said, "Look to the green,
son. Whenever you want to know why or why not, look for
the people who are making money off it."

It was a bit cynical, but his advice holds true in many cases.
If you want to understand why something is as it is, consider
who's making money from the status quo. Or who stands to
lose money if the problem is suddenly fixed.

Would the drug companies welcome a cure for the common cold? What would they do with their multibillion-dollar
market in nasal spray, pain killers, sinus aids, facial tissue,
cough drops, and antihistamines? Did the razor company
rave over the final solution to shaving? No way. Do slum
lords want an end to slums? Do arms merchants want an end
to the Soviet threat? Do dentists want an end to toothaches?

Get Past the Thought Barrier

Here lies a significant lesson: *New ideas, innovations, and
better solutions have to fight to survive.* They have to overcome vested interests, forces of habit, and entrenched prejudices to become real. And this sends us on to the Pathway of
Innovation, getting past good ideas to actual results, real improvement. Listening and prospecting give us the information and meaning we need to save ourselves, but we're not

safe until we get past the "thought barrier" and into the next realm, the world of action. So far you've learned to take it all in and make sense of it. Now it's time to put it to work. It's time to innovate.

PictoGame—Round 2

If the previous pictograms helped round out the barriers to listening, try looking over the ones below and on the next page. They illustrate mistakes made on the Prospect Pathway, common errors shown in graphic format. See if you can decipher a failed technique or a barrier for each one. Then check the answers I came up with at the end of the book. Who knows, your interpretation might be better than mine.

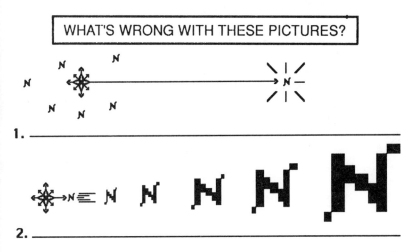

WHAT'S WRONG WITH THESE PICTURES?

1. ─────────────────────────────────

2. ─────────────────────────────────

(Continued)

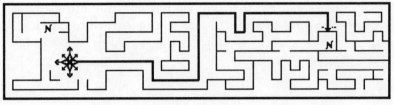

3. _____

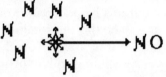

4. _____

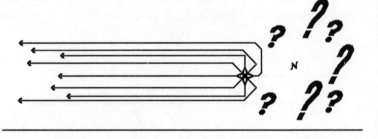

5. _____

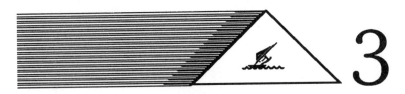

3

Break Away
From Convention

*Innovation isn't doing things better. It's
doing things differently, with better results.*

The *Innovate* Pathway

The Sex of Business _____

Mentioning innovation to contemporary executives is like
mentioning sex to prison inmates: You've got their attention.
But what is this magic process so prized by today's companies? *Process* is the key word here. In this chapter I'll take
you behind the veil that lies between the results of innovation
and the processes that bring it into being. Innovation is so
rare and so valuable because only a few people know how it's
done. You have to think differently and act on those
thoughts differently. I'll show you how this is done. I'll show
you how to innovate.

    Innovation is difficult to define but easy to recognize. It's
easy to see innovative products once they've been introduced,

to recognize the *results* of innovation. But few of us know the *workings* of innovation: how someone came up with the idea in the first place. It's hard to put our finger on the ingredients, the way of thinking or the process of conceiving and producing something everyone knows is innovative as soon as it's seen.

The Quick Innovation Quiz

Let's test your current way of thinking to see if there's a latent innovator hiding within you. Answer the following ten questions with either a yes (if you agree with the statement) or no (if you disagree).

	Yes	*No*
1. People above me know more than I do.	____	____
2. Great ideas aren't necessarily innovations.	____	____
3. Innovators are geniuses.	____	____
4. I was born to innovate.	____	____
5. To get ahead you must learn the rules.	____	____
6. People do a lot of work that's unnecessary.	____	____
7. Most of the easy discoveries have been made.	____	____
8. Sometimes less is more.	____	____
9. You've got to be technical to innovate.	____	____
10. Doing things differently is fun.	____	____

Now count up your score. For every even-numbered question that you answered with yes, give yourself ten points. For every odd-numbered question you answered with no, give yourself another ten points. A perfect score is 100. Write your score here: _____ . If it's less than 60, you need to re-think what innovation is. You could be restricting your natural talents and denying yourself the pleasures and rewards of innovation. If your score was higher than 60, you've got a good idea of what innovation is, but you could still use some help in finding out how to innovate. In either case, following the Innovate Pathway will lead to more innovation, more frequently and more quickly. In this chapter we'll look at how some innovative products and services came about and learn key skills you'll use to innovate from now on.

Innovation Isn't Rocket Science

What's the source of innovation? Can it be taught? Do you have to be a rocket scientist to be innovative, or are there fundamental tricks that the innovative know and we don't? First, understand that it doesn't take a genius. Some of the most innovative ideas were dreamed up by uneducated, unsophisticated, and simple people. Take the paper clip. Some guy probably just twisted a piece of wire during his spare time, maybe when he was daydreaming or just had to do something with his hands. Presto! The most ubiquitous office product in the world appeared. Pretty low-tech too.

The Genius Behind the Walkman

Or what about the famous Sony Walkman radios and tape players? When they came out in the early eighties, the entire industrial world jumped on them, and the business press made Akio Morita, Sony's chairman, into an instant genius. But think about the product itself. I remember buying my first transistor radio as a kid in the fifties. It was a Sears Silvertone, probably made in Japan, of course, but it was essentially the same as the Walkman that would win acclaim thirty years later as one of the most innovative products on earth. How could my fifties' transistor have cost $9.95 (with a leather case) and Morita's brainstorm go for over a hundred bucks, during the same time when all electronics prices were plummeting? What happened?

All Sony did was attach two earpieces to the radio instead of one. They already had stereo receivers, everybody did. They simply tied two earpiece speakers to the radio, one for each channel. Doesn't seem too complicated to me. But it made all the difference. It rejuvenated consumer electronics, and even the social scientists, urban scholars, and philosophers have written about the eventual effects. People were now "cocooning while commuting," "walking in their own worlds" (and stepping out in front of trucks).

I was working in Japan at the time they first came out. My American partners were buying them up by the suitcaseful and bringing them back to the States to resell at a premium. We all recognized the result: something that would sell big. But what about the process that led up to it? Was it a market survey, a strategic plan, a global financial study? Or was it something a little more simple?

I can just hear some engineer deep in the bowels of Sony coming up with the idea. "Hey, people have two ears, but our radios only have one earphone. Why not make an earphone for the other ear?" From what seemed like a simple, even naive question, a social, economic, and financial phenomenon arose to rock the world. Sony didn't call a bunch of execs together, hire consultants, research the market, or consider the socioeconomic impacts. They just made some and sent them out to stores. The rest is business-success history. Innovation can be simple. It's the results that can be stunning.

You Were Born to Innovate

Innovation is nothing more than taking what you have, or can get quickly, and using it to get what you want. Even infants are innovative. When my son was 18 months old, he had a habit of putting his hands in his food and drawing "strained-pea" diagrams on the wall. After his hands were slapped a few times, he stopped being innovative. But really, all he was doing was using what was at hand, literally, to make something that he wanted: a picture. He could have been a guest lecturer at Harvard Business School. He had something going for him that many of us don't. He was naive, ignorant, and untrained. These are key characteristics of the innovative.

Slap Back at the Handslappers

As you learn more about the process of innovation, you'll realize how essential these traits can be. And you'll discover that most of us have had our hands slapped enough times to kill whatever natural inclination toward innovation we started out with. Schools, parents, universities, job experiences, and the like are designed to stifle innovation by regimenting us, making us pay more attention to the rules than the results, and shaming into ignoring what seems obvious as "too simple" or telling us "if it was such a good idea, someone would have thought of it before." I don't think the engineer at Sony, the person behind the phenomenon of the Walkman, was the first one to realize that people had two ears. It seemed simple. It was. And that's why it was so innovative.

Unlearning to Innovate

I want you to learn how to innovate by following the example set by that engineer, and by the wire twister who dreamed up the paper clip and the infant behind the pea Picassos. What stops most of us from learning how to be innovative is that it's more an "unlearning" than a learning effort. We've got to forget, ignore, avoid, and sometimes disobey the unwritten rules, assumptions, guidelines, and standards that have been crammed into our heads since we were facing a jar of strained peas ourselves. Innovation is inside you. I'm going

to help you let it out. I'm going to teach you how to turn what
seems simple into something stunning.

Ignore the Voice Inside You _____

The biggest problem with innovation is that we're taught not
to do it. We're taught to fall in line, keep our mouths shut, obey,
conform, and follow. And the insidious part is that, after 20 or
30 years of this, we're censoring ourselves. We end up with a
small voice inside us that takes the place of the parents, teachers, cops, priests, and bosses even when they're not around.
You've heard this voice from time to time, I'm sure. It's the one
that says, "Naaaa…that's too simple," or "Naaaa…I'll look stupid if I mention this." If you really want to be innovative, if you
want to share the success and the glory that pours forth on even
the most humble innovator, the first step is to stifle that voice.
It's been stifling you for too long.

Why Didn't I Think of That? _____

Innovation is like art, or maybe pornography. We don't know
what it is, but we know it when we see it. Whether it's a product or service or just a smarter way of doing things, there
isn't a woman or man among us that doesn't want to say,
"Why didn't I think of that?" or "That's so simple it's a wonder no one ever thought of it before."

One reason most haven't is that we're so accustomed to unwritten rules and assumptions that it takes breaking them to
see how artificial they really are. Innovation is very different
from other methods of improvement. It's not winning by
learning the rules or following them with more diligence, but
by breaking them. To be innovative we must begin by forgetting or by deliberately putting conventional wisdom out of
our minds. Then we create the new rules.

Innovative products and services share common features.
They're usually simple, straightforward, and often lack

something every predecessor had. They come about when we focus on the results of a product or service and ignore its features. And they don't always require technological advances. Consider paper clips, overnight delivery, and the disposable pen.

Fast-Forward Innovation

The Innovate Pathway is at the heart of *fast-forward* thinking. It's quick, brings immediate results, and doesn't require years of training, special skills, or authorization from someone else. It's the prize at the end of the first two pathways: Listening and Prospecting. They help you find out what's going on, what's needed, and why. Innovation helps you turn that information into profit. It's the payoff for listeners and prospectors.

Keep in mind that you might not be inventing anything, or getting a patent, a copyright, or a franchise on the latest fad when you innovate. You might be winning in other, not so public ways. Like when you come up with a better way to keep track of spare parts in the warehouse, a faster way to bill customers, or a safer way to dispose of plastic waste in your factory. These might not make the headlines, but they eliminate waste, cut costs and improve profit, enhance working conditions, or promote quality. Who can argue against that?

Here are my five most important suggestions for would-be innovators.

1. *Act stupid.* Stupid people don't understand why something new can't be done. They ask *Why* often, and *Why not* continually. They innovate. Their minds roam freely, unrestricted by conventional wisdom.

2. *Ignore the rules.* Business rules deal with how things are to be done, how products "should" work, and what people "will" accept. If everything remains the same, the rules

prevail. But when customers' needs change, or technology, lifestyles, expectations, or processes change, the rules will be revised—not by the followers, but by the innovators.

3. *Baseball—nachos.* The actual term is *disassociate*, which means breaking those seemingly automatic links between things. Psychologists like to play word-association games to find out how people link thoughts together. But we inadvertently link products and services together when we don't have to. If you're playing the game and someone says "baseball," you might say "hot dogs" (or "apple pie"). But what if you said "nachos"? As it turns out, more people are buying nachos at some major league parks than hot dogs. Some innovator "disassociated," broke the links.

4. *Try it backwards.* Turn it upside down, move it upstream or downstream, or turn it inside out. These are the exercises of the innovative. They also ask, "Can we throw it away, make it into a toy, shrink it, or blow it up?" To those trapped by the rules, innovators are frightening.

5. *Try and see.* Ideas seldom sell, but products and services do. With innovation, the winner isn't someone who *thought of it first* but someone who *does it first.* If we wait until we have it perfect or until we study all implications, we may never have it. Innovators like to try.

Why It's Smart to Act Stupid

Let's face it, no one wants to look stupid. In school, we've all felt the flush of embarrassment when the rest of the class stares at us after we gave the wrong answer. We've all suffered the humiliation that comes when we speak too soon on a new job and our coworkers give us a look that says, "Where the hell is he coming from?" This is the reason that 99 percent of us are afraid to innovate. The very act of trying things differently or standing out among the rest subjects us to possible ridicule. But it's impossible to be successful without standing out, or without trying something new, or without being different. It goes with the territory. If you didn't want to be different, you wouldn't have bought this book. But how do you pull it off? How do you act stupid without appearing stupid?

To begin with, you act stupid silently. You allow yourself to consider things in your thoughts without having to prove them to yourself. When you question the rules, when you ask why, do it internally. If you can't come up with a sensible answer, then put the question to others. Have them justify things as they are. Have them explain why something should be as it is. If they start to stumble and mumble, you're on to something.

Play a Stupid Game With Stunning Results. Make it a game, like, "I understand the obvious reasons for cars to have spare tires, but can you think of a good reason for them not to have spare batteries, or spare fan belts?" After the discussion progresses a bit, you'll both be back to the spare tire issue. "Yeah, I can't remember the last time I had a flat tire on the highway. But I do recall having a fan belt break. Hey, I wonder if we could get rid of spare tires? That would save trunk space, production costs, and fuel." This is exactly the kind of thinking that led to the emergency spare, the inflatable spare, and the like. It has saved American motorists billions of dollars over the years and millions of barrels of imported oil. It was simple. The results were stunning.

But what if you question similar assumptions on your job? Suppose you act stupid by saying, "Why does the purchasing department have to get a copy of the marketing plan every time it's revised?" Don't let them stop you or cut you off with, "They always get a copy," or "That's the policy," or "They're on the distribution list." Probe deeper. Ask the follow-up question, like, "I wonder how many of the people who get a copy actually need one?"

What to Expect When You Act Stupid. Acting stupid means questioning what's done, why it's done, and how it's done. Don't use this technique without some caution. No one likes a continual pest or somebody who questions everything. Never ask why or why not without thinking through the answers yourself. Be ready for the follow-up. Be ready to make your point. Do all the open-ended questioning without speaking, in your own mind.

Also, be prepared for a *cascading effect*. That's when your question triggers a whole host of other questions. If the purchasing department might not need a copy of the marketing report, why does the legal staff need one? Or why does the purchasing department get copies of other reports? In fact, why does any group other than marketing need it? And so forth. Questioning is healthy and contagious. It tests assumptions that in turn leads to the testing of other assumptions. It's the first step on the Innovate Pathway.

And remember that innovation isn't just coming up with something new. It can also be getting rid of something old, outdated, or unneeded. There are two sides to innovation: coming up with what we need but don't have and alternatively, or at the same time, getting rid of something we have but don't need. You'll never know about either case unless you ask why or why not. That's acting stupid but being smart.

The world is full of consultants who are paid handsome fees for acting stupid. One client told me so. He said, "You come into our organization, ask our people 'why' about everything, write their answers in a report, and charge us several thousand dollars for telling us what we've told you." He was absolutely correct. I'm not sure whether he knew that that's why many consultants are hired. Top management wants to know what their people already know but are afraid to say. They're afraid to act stupid. As a consultant, I've been paid a lot of money for acting stupid. To me, that in itself seems smart.

Rules Are Made to Be Broken, or at Least Ignored

Businesses, governments, organizations of all types are full to the brim with rules. You see bookshelves groaning under the weight of dozens of manuals, procedures, policies, and standards. From Singapore to South Africa, I've written them, reviewed them, and revised them for my clients. And these are just the rules that are written down and published! An even greater number of rules deal with unwritten modes of behavior, assumed relationships, and what's done or not done around here. Even the most unbureaucratic, entrepreneurial outfits are rule-bound. What are all these rules for, anyway?

Robert Reich, a noted Harvard professor and social commentator, says that organizations exist so that a group can have fewer objectives than the sum of its members. In other words, organizations exist to focus the effort of a lot of people on a few goals. That makes sense. But it means rules dealing with what's done and what's not done. It means constraining behavior. It means that there's a good chance that a great idea will be stymied before it's born because somewhere and in some way it conflicts with the rules.

The $50-Million Permission Slip. During the early years of the oil crisis, consultants, construction companies, airlines, and all types of megacorporations were scrambling to get a piece of the action in the Middle East. Everybody could smell petrodollars in the robes of suddenly rich Arab sheiks. I was hired by a joint venture of an accounting firm and an international construction company. We spent three long months working 18-hour days putting together a lump-sum bid to computerize the transportation department of the Kingdom of Saudi Arabia. The proposal was awesome—several thick volumes, all of it according to their precise specifications. Everything was spelled out in minute detail for the 50 million dollars we bid. It was written in Arabic and English, had to be stamped by about twelve U.S. government officials, and we had sent several representatives to Saudi Arabia for pre-bid conferences. We'd put over a half million dollars into the proposal work, and our hopes were running high. We knew we were good, looked good on paper, and could do a good job. And we knew that if we got the job, we'd make a ton of money.

All the arrangements were made to have one of our guys carry the two footlockers of papers to Riyadh in his personal luggage. Flights were booked, people were waiting in Europe to take it on its final leg of the journey, and telexes and faxes were buzzing around the globe. There was great anticipation.

As my two associates wheeled the footlockers through the lobby of the firm's corporate headquarters in downtown Chicago, I ran outside to hail a cab. Time was extremely tight. The flight was scheduled to leave in 45 minutes and the airport was a good 30 minutes away. I paid the cabbie ten bucks to wait in the street outside the office. We sat there waiting for the footlockers. Nothing happened. Nobody came out of the building. In desperation I paid the cabbie more money and told him to wait a bit longer, then ran back into the lobby.

Standing next to my two associates, with a burly arm on the dolly carrying our 50-million-dollar paperwork, stood a security guard—a rent-a-cop. He wouldn't let them leave the building with a package like that unless they had written authorization from the building superintendent. He was adamant: No permission slip, no package outside. The guy was following the rules. It didn't matter that the man pushing the dolly was the partner in charge of the entire office. Or that his firm owned the building. Nope. No deal. He even drew his gun to make his point.

Through the glass I saw the cabbie growing impatient, ready to leave. In my mind I saw a 50-million-dollar deal going bye-bye, along with my fee. What to do? The building superintendent was out to lunch, so that wouldn't work. Finally, I ran to the bank of elevators off the lobby and asked my secretary to do something innovative. In a moment, she was screaming from an opened elevator, the guard was rushing to the elevator to rescue her, and I was loading two footlockers in the back of a cab. We sped away. Mission accomplished. Sometimes you have to break the rules. I got chewed out by the security guard. I also got paid enough to buy a new Jaguar. And the firm got the job. I hate rules. I love innovation…and dramatic secretaries.

Rules obstruct people, but you'd be surprised how often they obstruct entire companies. When you're told, "We don't do that," or "No company in this industry does that," you're hearing an opening for innovation. Because with competitive pressure as it is, the companies that win are the first ones to break the rules. Everyone else, caught off guard, then points at a successful company and says, "Hey, we could have done that too." But they didn't, mainly because they still assumed that everyone else was as hobbled by the unwritten rules as they were. Innovators aren't.

Batteries Not Included. One of my most memorable frustrations as a kid was getting some toy for Christmas that required batteries and not getting the batteries to work the damned thing. My parents never bothered to read the "batteries not included" notices on the toy boxes. I'm sure the makers of these toys couldn't care less, or that they "assumed" all parents were conscientious. Or they told themselves, We're in the toy truck business, not the battery business. That didn't help me all day Christmas as I looked at the toy and imagined how much fun it would be if it worked.

Here again the Japanese beat us at a simple trick. When you buy a Panasonic calculator, watch, radio, tape player, anything—they all come with Panasonic batteries in the package. Why? They want satisfied customers. And they know that if a customer can see it or hear it work in the store and it seems okay, he or she will buy the product. The psychiatrists call it "instant gratification." You don't have to trust that it'll work. You can tell it works, you get gratified, you buy it.

The Wrath of an Eight-Year-Old. Can't you just bet some Japanese marketing expert suffered through a Christmas with a toy that wouldn't work? And when told that "we don't make batteries, and besides that, no other electronics companies package batteries with their equipment," he went into a fit. He ignored the rules, the company sold a zillion more gadgets, and the customers liked them. The guy who suggested that batteries be included surely wasn't a rocket scientist—just a grown-up who never forgot a quiet radio or a motionless truck from his childhood. Don't underestimate the wrath, or the memory, of a disappointed eight-year-old. A footnote: I just bought my teenage daughter a new Nissan sports car. We lifted the hood and, you guessed it, a Panasonic battery.

Even God Stopped at Ten Commandments.   Always question the rules. Always remember that even God wrote only ten commandments. The rest of the rules were written, or assumed, by mere mortals. God never wrote that dogs aren't allowed to eat ice cream (Frosty Paws, a big hit at today's supermarkets) or that you can't eat your breakfast eggs with your fingers (Egg McMuffin, the forerunner of an explosion in fast-food breakfasting). And God never said you had to eat a hot dog at the ballpark. But that's the next story.

Word Disassociation _____

All of us go to ball games, movies, concerts, and other public events. And if you are a good listener, and a smart prospector, you'll notice something most people don't. Most of the food that you buy is shared food. I mean, most of it is something more than one person can eat at the same time. Take popcorn. How many times do you see a couple, three friends, or a parent and child sitting in a movie theater each with his or her own box of popcorn. Doesn't happen very often. Instead, you see them sharing a big box. It may seem hard to believe, but trust me. Innovation is at work here.

First, consider that most people go to these events in groups: family members, friends, dates, spouses, and so forth. Are you going to attend and get something just for yourself? Are you going to get some popcorn and not offer it to your date, your husband, or your roommate? Of course not, but what do you do when you go to a baseball game? Do you pass the hot dog down the row and let the whole family chomp off a bite? Too gross, you say, too messy? Well, now you understand why hot dogs shouldn't be a big hit at stadiums. Were it not for tradition and a few singles who attend, they'd be obsolete. The only reason we have them is to satisfy childhood memories or because back in the roaring twenties, or whenever, they didn't have popcorn, nachos, pizza, and fajitas. So the hot dog stays. But nachos are creeping into their turf. Because nachos are shared food—easy to pass around, easy to share.

Making Big Bucks From Chicken Feed. How else would you explain the popularity of popcorn at movie theaters? After all, considering the amazing variety of today's snack foods, popcorn is just one step away from animal feed. But, it's a shared food. Now when someone says "movies," you say "popcorn," and when they say "baseball," you say "hot dogs." But some enterprising theater owners are getting wise. They know the value added to popcorn by popping it doesn't pay much. I don't care how large the tub (and they are getting gargantuan nowadays), you can only charge so much for heated animal feed. So, enter high-value-added "sharefood": nachos with cheese, chili, sour cream, whatever you like. Now when dad takes the kids to see the show, he spends twelve bucks on snacks instead of two-fifty. Now the cycle is almost broken. When today's kids hear the word *popcorn*, they don't automatically say "movie," they say "huh?" or "microwave!"

I think word association, and subsequent disassociation, are marvelous *fast-forward* tools. You can use them to find and destroy unwritten assumptions galore. Innovators do this all the time. If you say "poolroom," they don't say "gambling, booze, and low-life." They say "malls, dates, yogurt." If you say, "shipping stuff to mom for Christmas," they don't say "post office." They say "franchised, shopping-center packaging services." If you say, "I threw away my razor, my fountain pen, my watch, my charcoal grill, my picnic cooler, my baby's pants, and my camera," they don't say "Leaving town?" They say, "So you finally discovered disposable products." And if you're talking to a kid, any kid in the free world, and say "Michelangelo," you won't hear "Renaissance artist," you'll hear "teenage mutant ninja turtle!"

Backward Is Best

I once had a neighbor we jokingly referred to as Backwards Bill. The man would cut his grass when it was pitch dark and paint his house when it was snowing. He'd put asphalt sealer, black and gooey, on his concrete driveway. He planted his tomato garden in his frontyard and kept his backyard well manicured. We all considered him crazy, eccentric, and just plain weird. When my grandmother would visit and stay in an upstairs bedroom, she'd peer out the window at Bill's shenanigans across the street. At least twice a day she'd holler down at us. "Have you seen what that man is up to now?" she'd say. Yes, Grannie, we know. That's Bill.

I never found out what Bill did for a living, but I think he should have been giving seminars to business people. Subject: Innovation. Whether he knew it or not, Bill was giving his neighbors a message: Break out of your old habits; try things differently—like backwards, for example, or upside down, or inside out.

Try this. Take a shirt or blouse and put it on inside out. Presto! You have a designer shirt. Isn't that what Polo, Izod, Liz Claiborne, Calvin Klein, and all the other high-priced clothing looks like? The labels are on the outside. You achieve a similar effect when your no-name shirt is reversed.

Or what if your company paid customers to buy your products or use your services? Sound backwards? Consider the airlines' frequent flier programs, automobile rebates, cash back when you use the Discover card?

More Backward Ideas.   Here are some examples that give further evidence that Backwards Bill is making an impact.

Can you imagine how stupid these suggestions would have seemed in a corporate boardroom just a few months or years ago?

"Let's brag about what our product doesn't have!"

Are you kidding? Conventional wisdom says brag about what your stuff has and don't mention what it doesn't. But I dare you to buy any packaged food product today that doesn't brag about being low in sodium, low in cholesterol, saturated fats, alcohol, sugar, palm oils, calories, caffeine. Or that doesn't say it's lacking in preservatives, additives, and artificial colors or flavors. Things are selling for what they don't have.

"Let's sell something that makes what's expensive look cheap!"

Seems backwards, doesn't it? I mean, shouldn't we be selling something that makes what's cheap look expensive? But not necessarily so. One of the strangest yet successful products at a recent consumer electronics show in Chicago was a $9.95 piece of plastic that made the front of your BMW's ultraexpensive compact disc player/stereo look like a cheap, Detroit-model AM radio. You stick the facade on to deter would-be stereo thieves. Now BMW (and others) are putting this expensive gear in the trunk, out of sight. Can you imagine that the next step is for someone to sell expensive-looking, plastic radio fronts for the dashboard so thieves won't break into your trunk to get the real thing?

"Let's sell pain!"

This runs totally against every sales pitch I've heard and every sales seminar I've attended. We sell things to ease pain, remove pain, blunt pain. But have you looked at television ads for health spas? Everyone is groaning and sweating and grimacing as they twist, lift, and push mechanical devices that look like updated apparatuses from the basement of the Marquis de Sade. Even Jane Fonda tells us to "feel it burn," and Cher reminds us, "If there's no pain, there's no gain." And think about this principle next time you watch a commercial for the U.S. Marine Corps. You won't hear the normal advertising hype like, "It's fun, it's easy, anyone can do it." What you'll hear is, "It's challenging, it's tough as hell, it may not be for you." It works.

"Let's watch music!"

For me, music has always been something to listen to. When I love an idea, I say it's "music to my ears." I can just hear my teenagers saying, "I like your idea, Scott. Why, it's music to my eyes." Yep, thank MTV and music videos for the transformation of music from an aural to a visual experience. When we're riding in the car and the radio is playing, my kids will say something like, "Is this the song where he's being chased by a pack of wolves, or is it the one where he's jumping out of people's heads?"

"Let's tell people not to buy our products!"

This wouldn't go over too well at a K-mart stockholder's meeting. But I remember working in Chicago and hearing that the Gucci store on Michigan Avenue was closing during lunch hour to keep the secretaries and other working women from shopping there. And we've all seen Avia sporting shoes advertised with the message that "our shoes are not for everyone," and "don't buy these shoes unless you're a serious athlete," or words to that effect. I can guess what happened. Every couch potato who wanted to look really fit headed for the Avia store. I wonder how they decided whether someone could buy the shoes? Did they put them on a treadmill first, and what if they failed? Did they send them to the Nike store?

"Let's sell a shoe that's not a shoe!"

This is what might happen if the couch potatoes failed the Avia workout test. They'd go to Nike and find their popular "nonshoe," technically a "racing sock." Yes, indeed. To strip all the unnecessary weight off a running shoe, Nike got down to what, in effect, is a nylon mesh upper with a rubberized strip of a sole. It looks like a sock and weighs about as much. Some people swear by them. They are the epitome of the Backwards Bill design philosophy. They made a shoe that really was a sock. And they even call this shoe a sock. It sells too. Nike is socking it to their competitors.

"Let's sell sand to the Saudi Arabians!"

It's true. Eskimos do buy ice cream and refrigerators, and the Saudi Arabians buy sand. Their sand isn't fit for most concrete mixes; it's not the right kind of sand. So to build their highways, airports, high rises, and bridges, they have been importing sand for years. I wouldn't doubt if Backwards Bill has the franchise.

Try and See

Twenty-five years ago a man named Hoyle Schweitzer stood on a surfboard while holding a sail in his hands. The worldwide, Olympic sport of windsurfing was born that day. I don't expect Schweitzer theorized much about the combination of a sail and a board, or if he had to defend the prospect in meetings or explain why it was a good idea to his peers or superiors. He just jumped on the board, stuck the sail in the wind, and said to himself, Holy cow! This is fantastic!

A lot of people might have thought of the idea before him. But nobody *did* it. That's the key difference between speculation and innovation. It's easier to think of things than to try them out and see if they work. But if you can't make it past the "thought barrier" to the action stage, you can't innovate. People won't buy theories, they buy things. They don't applaud good speculation, they praise good service.

The Joy of Just Doing It. If Schweitzer had followed conventional wisdom, he'd probably still be playing with models in a wind tunnel, or researching what the Japanese were doing in water sports. Then when someone else came out with the sailboard, he'd be quite justified in saying, "Gee, I thought of that before they did." But you don't innovate by thinking alone. You innovate by doing.

Here's why so few of us innovate on a regular basis. When our ideas are just that, ideas, they are easy to criticize, ridicule, or laugh off. But when they're a physical reality, they stand on their own. Everybody can put forth a counterargument for every great idea you come up with. Ideas and arguments are dirt cheap. They're easy targets. You've got to get beyond the idea stage quickly. *Fast-forward* innovation means getting to working models, prototypes, or demonstrations ASAP.

I've heard it over and over: "Well, I never thought I would like it, but once I saw it in operation, it looked pretty good"; or, "It does seem different (or silly, or simple, or weird), but how can you argue with success?"

You must force yourself to follow your hunches, ideas, and dreams. You must get beyond speculation and get specific, tangible results. To keep you moving toward a real innovation and not just a good idea, remember these points:

1. *Nothing is perfect.* Everything can be improved, except those things that aren't developed. Fix the bugs, and add the bells and whistles later.

2. *Some people can find fault with the Mona Lisa.* They'll jump all over what you propose or what you've done. It has nothing to do with you, your work, or your product or idea. It probably occurs because they just lost money at the racetrack, are getting a divorce, hate the color green, or are always in a bitchy mood when the moon is full.

3. *You can't prove, disprove, or judge ideas.* Don't fall into the trap of playing the "what-if" game until you see the innovative result. Let the customer judge.

Think about some innovative products people have spent good money on recently. Would you have invested anything in a guy who proposed to package rocks in gift boxes and sell them in department stores? Are you kidding? But once you saw them in the stores and saw people laying out good money for Pet Rocks, chances are you told yourself, "Seems silly, but how can you argue with success?"

What if you were asked to support the idea of a disposable camera? I can think of a hundred reasons why it wouldn't make sense. I'd point out the cost of the lenses, the electronics, the mechanical parts, the case, strap, battery, and everything else that goes into a standard 35-mm camera. But once I saw one and paid five bucks for it, including film, I was a convert. Fuji redefined the camera. It went from "complicated, engineered precision equipment" to "plastic film holder with hole in front." Kodak raced a competitive product (the Fling) to the market. They probably would have turned down the idea if one of their people suggested it. But once they *saw* it, they knew it was terrific. So did everybody else. Fuji *made* it first. They won. They innovated.

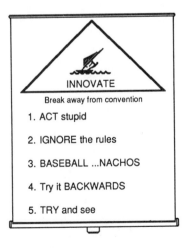

INNOVATE

Break away from convention

1. ACT stupid

2. IGNORE the rules

3. BASEBALL ...NACHOS

4. Try it BACKWARDS

5. TRY and see

P. S.—The World Is Full of Wanna-Be's _____

One final note before we get to the "innovation blockers." The world is full of people who "could be," "wanna be," or "will be." But the winners are the ones who just "be," the ones who try it and see. In my lectures, interviews, and consulting experience I commonly run into typical questions regarding the writing of a book. People want to know how long it takes, how you get started, and where you came up with the concept. Inevitably, one of them will make a comment that sends me into a fit of rage. Something like, "Yeah, well, I've been thinking about writing a book myself. I could if I wanted to. I just don't have the time." If you ever want to irritate an author, say that to him or her. It's sort of like saying, "What you've done is easy—anybody could do it." Always remember that royalties accrue to the one who writes the book, not the one who could have written it.

If I do nothing more in this chapter than impress on you the importance of trying, of doing rather than thinking about or talking about your idea, I'll have succeeded. I want you to employ *fast-forward* techniques so you can leave the herd of "could be's" and join the much smaller group of successful innovators. Talk is cheap, ideas are plentiful. But innovative products and services can be priceless. Try and see.

Barriers to Breaking Away From Convention

Whoever said that tennis balls had to be white, that computers belonged in the data processing department, or that milk had to be delivered in bottles? It wasn't a person, but the nemesis of innovation: conventional wisdom. It's funny how conventional wisdom can become unconventional wisdom so quickly, how what was smart becomes kind of stupid as soon as someone demonstrates the power of unconventional thought and looks at things differently.

Rules, regulations, tradition, rigid control, uniformity, and conformity—all stifle innovation. If innovation has any rule, it's this: There are no rules. When you stop accepting everything as it is, the barriers to innovation start to fall away. The innovation blockers crumble. What are they?

1. Someone Must Have... Assuming that it must have been tried before is the first mistake you can make. The world isn't full of innovators constantly trying new products or services. There are more answers than askers. Don't discount your own insight. And just because they might have thought of it—did they do it? Or did they stop at another barrier?

2. If It Isn't Broken...Don't Fix It. Another excuse for inaction. Excellence requires constant improvement. There is no final, perfect product or method. A better saying might be, "If it isn't being fixed, it's broken."

3. Paralysis by Analysis. Or studying it to death. Or forming a committee, a review board, or a research project. This is the flip side to jumping to conclusions. It's jumping *from* conclusions. If we wait long enough, or study it enough, there will always be a reason not to. Conventional wisdom will win.

4. Punishment for Failure. Excessive punishment for failure is the greatest barrier of all. It expects perfection on the first try. Pretty soon people give up. We need to redefine failure, from "not being successful" to "not trying." Babe Ruth led the league in strikeouts. Nobody punished him. Nobody points to Fuji's disposable camera and says, "What a cheap, low-tech piece of junk. Any idiot could operate that!" Fuji knew that one of the primary factors in the decision NOT to buy a camera was that they appear too complex. The world is full of potential customers, so-called "idiots" who don't want to become professional photographers. They just want to have a picture of Fluffy when she comes home from the dog groomer. They love the benefits of the camera, but couldn't care less about its features.

5. Loving Features, Forgetting Benefits. Features are the characteristics of a product or service, but they aren't its benefits. To focus on what something is, how it works, or its components is often to neglect what it is *for*—what it does. People buy what it does more than what it is. If you love the features but forget why they exist, you're blocking innovation. Change the features to give the same or better benefits. That's innovating.

1. SOMEONE must have...

2. If it isn't BROKEN...

3. PARALYSIS by analysis

4. PUNISHMENT for failure

5. Loving FEATURES,
   forgetting BENEFITS

Innovation by Elimination

On my desk as I type this are three writing pens: a Mont Blanc Diplomat (price: $250), a Papermate ballpoint (about $3.95), and a Bic Stik (9 cents when you buy them in a bag by the dozen). All write well. All achieve the same purpose or benefit: markings on paper. When Bic created the Stik years ago, they looked at a Papermate-type conventional pen and said, What can we take away from this and still have the end result—markings on paper? They removed all the springs, gears, cogs, threaded parts, and connections that make up a refillable click-type pen. They ended up with the point and the ink tube. They rolled this tube in plastic, pressed a cheap cap out of more plastic, and put the result on the market. They call this design principle the "Bauhaus principle" or "less is more." Bic innovated by taking away all the features that didn't contribute to the bare benefits of the product. That's innovation: taking away what you have but don't need—innovation by elimination.

But how do you explain the popularity of the very expensive, cumbersome, nonutilitarian Mont Blanc pens? Simple. They have a very different benefit, a different purpose. It's not markings on paper, but "fashion accessory." They are status symbols, wardrobe enhancers, or whatever. But they aren't intended just to write. You could get a Stik and do the same. But few of us want to show up for a presentation before the board of directors with a Bic Stik jutting out of our shirt pocket. Focus on the purpose, the ultimate and singular benefit of everything you do or make. Strip away everything that doesn't materially contribute to that benefit. You'd be surprised how much can be tossed out, eliminated, or forgotten.

Dreams Come True, Sometimes

I frequently use pens and pencils as examples of *fast-forward* techniques for a couple of reasons. First, they're easy to carry around and use for lecture props, and, secondly, I guess I've always had a thing for them. When I was a child, we had little money, and I had to stretch each pencil as far as it would go. I'd whittle on them with a butter knife to get a point because they were so small that if I put them into a pencil sharpener at school, they'd get swallowed up and I couldn't get them out. While other kids dreamed of owning a go-cart or a pony, I had my heart set on a brand new, No. 2, school-bus-yellow Faber-Castell, one with a flat end and a virgin eraser! Wow! If I only had one of those!

My mother and her five children were down on our luck back then and were renting out an empty ward in an army hospital. We lived down the hall from the psychiatric ward, the orthopedic ward, and the laboratory. My two brothers and I sold newspapers to the patients to make ends meet. One day we were walking down the hospital corridor when we spied an orderly pushing a supply cart. He rounded a corner and a small, cardboard box slid inadvertently off the cart. Once he was gone, the three of us started fighting over the box, not knowing what it contained. My middle brother got to it first. He ripped open the lid and found 144 brand new, yellow pencils inside! Eureka! Dreams do come true. We got enough to supply each of us through high school!

Surprise Package! _____

Two weeks later, while walking down another corridor, we came upon yet another cardboard box. It was identical to the pencil box, and we immediately started fighting again to see who would get all the pencils. My oldest brother won and gleefully leapt on the box. He ripped open the lid in triumph—the victor getting the spoils. Inside, however, he didn't find 144 yellow pencils. He found a stool specimen!

Is there a management principle in all this? Of course. In fact, there are two: (1) Don't fight over something you don't know about, and (2) Sometimes you may think you've lost, but you've really won.

The World's Best Innovators (It Takes a Thief)

I've said that innovation is natural, that we're all born to innovate, and that most of us get so regimented and conditioned that innovation is "learned" out of us. But of all the people from different walks of life I've met, some are better than others. Do engineers, artists, or teachers make better innovators? How about doctors, welders, or accountants? People in any field, with any education have the potential to innovate. There are no entrance examinations, licenses, or training programs you must complete.

Anybody can innovate, even thieves. In fact, thieves and other criminals are natural innovators. They're the best. By nature, they break the rules, ignore them, or don't even know them. They use what they have to get what they want. They don't worry about ridicule, embarrassment, or failure. They don't have that voice inside them which tells others like you or me, "Naaa...I'll look foolish if I suggest that." They don't even care if someone has done it before. And they have that natural bias toward action. They don't think about it, plan it, test it, or study it through a committee. They just do it.

The Case of the Missing Nickels

When I was a kid living in the hospital, I loved to drop a nickel into an old Coke machine and get a bottle at the end of the day. One day I put in a treasured quarter, got the bottle, and heard four plunks inside the machine. But four nickels' change did not appear in the coin-return slot. I was furious, slammed the machine a few times, and went off grumbling to my oldest brother. He came back with me later, put in another quarter, got his Coke, and heard the same four plunks. No change. What a rip-off!

But he didn't kick the machine or curse it. He thought for a while, then put his small fingers way up the coin-return opening and gingerly pulled something out. It was a cigarette box, carefully folded, absolutely full of nickels. Some thief had jammed it up there to collect everyone's change, and presumably would return periodically to harvest our nickels. Ingenious! Bad, wrong, illegal, to be sure. But I never would have thought of such a scam. The unknown thief didn't try to rip off the machine. He was ripping off the machine's customers! The machine owners would never miss a nickel or suspect anything. The customers would simply chalk it up to a faulty machine. What a deal!

Someone finally figured it out, and the newer machines were made with a one-way hinge to keep probing fingers out of the interior. Incidentally, I never did understand how my brother figured this trick out. But doesn't this illustrate innovation? Don't thieves have something to teach us?

Bricks and Pillowcases: The Tools of Innovation

My daughter's friend woke recently to find her new car up on bricks in her driveway—minus wheels. The thieves simply grabbed paving bricks that made up the driveway and supported the car with stacks of them until they removed the wheels and left. I would have worried about carrying four jacks, leaving my jacks, making noise with the jacks, and a whole host of other considerations. Or I'd have been looking for ways to carry a hundred bricks in my car, if I were a thief. These crooks simply grabbed the bricks from the driveway, right under the car. They brought nothing, invested nothing, and took off with everything! Pretty innovative.

When I returned home from vacation and found my house burglarized, I learned that the thief had used a pillowcase off my bed to store and transport my jewelry, silverware, and other small valuables. I never would have thought of that. Had I been the burglar, I'd have followed the rules. The rules say that pillowcases are for covering pillows. I would have searched throughout the house looking for a proper bag or box. I'd still be standing in the kitchen thinking, If I lived here, where would I store my trash bags? when the police cruiser roared up the driveway. Don't get me wrong. Innovation isn't theft, and crime is wrong. But you can learn from the strangest sources. You can learn to be innovative from thieves.

More Proaction Tips and Tricks

I've got more ideas for you than can fit in neat categories. Here I'd like to present some further suggestions to get you on the pathway of innovation. The first deals with your innate ability to innovate and what might be keeping you from tapping into it.

You don't have to be good to be great.

This might sound paradoxical, but some of the best musicians in the world can't read music, some of the most revered artists can't draw beyond stick figures, and the record stores are full of titles by people who can't sing. If Jackson Pollock were to have stopped painting because he couldn't draw representational figures, the world would be without some of the finest abstract art created. Pollock revolutionized painting. He created masterpieces by dripping, splattering, and slopping paint directly from cans onto canvases laid out on the floor. His work is known and treasured worldwide. Students and critics universally admire his technique. But he didn't touch a brush or a pencil. You don't have to be a great drawer to be a great painter. Pollock might have practiced our word-disassociation rule. When someone said "paint," he didn't say "brush"; he said "can."

The Beatles produced over 170 songs and took the global music scene by storm. Their influence is everywhere, and at one time their records accounted for a whopping 60 percent of all U.S. music sales. But John Lennon and Paul McCartney couldn't read or write music. You don't have to write music to create some of the best music the world has ever heard.

When Jimi Hendrix, a legendary guitarist and rocker of the psychedelic era, first started as a back-up player for blues and soul musicians, he was incredibly shy about his own talents, particularly his inability to sing well. One of his life's revelations occurred when he listened to his first Bob Dylan song. For the first time, Hendrix realized that you don't have to sing like Johnny Mathis or Frank Sinatra to be a singer. The rest is rock-and-roll history. Hendrix learned that you don't have to be able to carry a tune to sell millions of albums. It was like he'd just been given permission to excel. And he did.

Heed the lessons of these innovators. Don't think you can't do something because you haven't been trained to do it. In fact, what's so illuminating about these figures is that their very inability to perform in conventional ways led directly to their unconventional, innovative, and stunning performances. Since they couldn't follow the rules, they made new rules. Now people are trying to paint like Jackson Pollock, write songs like Lennon and McCartney, and perform on stage like Jimi Hendrix. Innovators break the rules, make new ones, and let the rest of the world take notes.

You can make a living doing anything.

One of the welcome pleasures of frequent air travel is that you sit next to people with the strangest jobs. You listen to their stories and leave the plane thinking, I had no idea people could make a living at that. I've met people who create computer programs for investors to track their wine collections, who specialize in cleaning houses after they've been damaged by fire, or teach ministers how to arrange the church's interior lighting for maximum effect. Everybody has a niche. I'm sure no parent tells their child that they want them to grow up and become a wine-inventory software designer. Yet if we listened to our parents, teachers, ministers, coaches, and the like, we'd all be doctors and lawyers. And none of us would be able to keep track of our wine collections!

Almost every leading figure in recent history took a sharp turn away from what others expected of him or her. Fyodor Dostoyevsky was sent to the Russian military academy and spent time in the artillery. If he'd followed the advice of others, there might have been a few more accurate cannonballs hurled over the steppes, but the world would be without *Crime and Punishment* and *The Brothers Karamazov*, not to mention the rest of his literary legacy. What if Albert Einstein had listened to those who said, "Look, young man, you've got a good, stable government job with a lot of benefits. Stick to it."? He'd have retired from the Swiss patent office as superclerk, and the theories of relativity would have to be discovered by someone else, maybe centuries later.

Each of us needs change to grow, improve, and progress.

Innovation is the act of changing outside the boundaries to growth, in spite of the regulations against progress, and regardless of the security that following the rules provides.

Go on the attack.

Why is it that innovators always have to defend what's new, and others don't have to justify what's old? Don't assume that things are done as they are because there's a good reason for it. There's always a reason, but it could be habit, tradition, sloppiness, carelessness, or just lack of imagination. Those are reasons, but not good reasons. Shift the burden of defense to those who accept what is. Go on the attack. And don't assume that "someone up there" at a higher level in your organization knows more than you do. One thing I've learned as I've moved upward in large organizations is that so many of those "up there" don't know so much after all, especially about what's going on "down here." You know the most about your job, what you do, and how it can be improved. Put that special knowledge to work.

Putting the Innovation Pathway to Use

Start by questioning everything you see, hear, or know. Make a list of the hidden assumptions about a particular product, process, or way of doing things. List any rules, written or unwritten, that don't seem to make sense or don't have to be. Take the five innovation techniques I've given you here and try them, one by one, on that product or way of working. Ask yourself, What would a visitor from another planet think about this? (Act Stupid.) Try it backwards, upside down, inside out. But be sure to try it.

Also examine the innovation blockers described in this chapter. For each one, ask yourself or your coworkers, "Is this stopping or delaying a great idea?" or "What features do

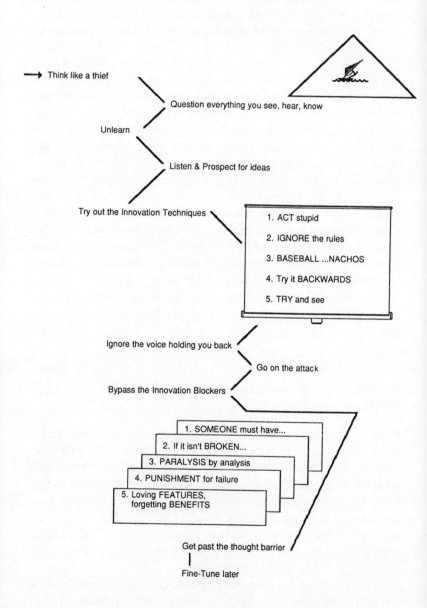

Think like a thief

Question everything you see, hear, know

Unlearn

Listen & Prospect for ideas

Try out the Innovation Techniques

1. ACT stupid

2. IGNORE the rules

3. BASEBALL ...NACHOS

4. Try it BACKWARDS

5. TRY and see

Ignore the voice holding you back

Go on the attack

Bypass the Innovation Blockers

1. SOMEONE must have...

2. If it isn't BROKEN...

3. PARALYSIS by analysis

4. PUNISHMENT for failure

5. Loving FEATURES, forgetting BENEFITS

Get past the thought barrier

Fine-Tune later

we have that don't contribute directly to the value of this thing, this activity, or this situation?"

And don't forget to keep listening and prospecting. Look for innovative products or activities everywhere you can. See if you can tell what makes them so special, so different. Do they break rules, do they disassociate, are they something old and simply turned inside out, upside down, or backwards? Look for ways to get your great ideas beyond the "thought barrier" and into reality. Make a model, draw a diagram of a new way to work, outline the benefits that won't be lost by radically reshaping, redirecting, or redesigning something. And don't forget to think like a thief, to ignore that voice that's inside and keeping you from innovating.

That's how you can practice innovation. Start by recognizing it all around you, then look at likely candidates and try these techniques on them. Think about the innovation blockers working against you, and use the techniques and ideas here to blast through them.

Finally, take five minutes to scan this chapter again. See if you agree that most of what you've learned is simple, quick, and almost second nature. That the skills to innovate are inside you, and have been for a long time. That you don't have to be a magician to perform some magic tricks yourself. You just have to recognize and reclaim these perceptions and skills. You have to dig them out from under all those rules, assumptions, restrictions, and norms that have been piling up since you were born. Innovation starts by unlearning. If you can learn to unlearn, you'll be headed down the Innovate Pathway. You'll be moving fast, and moving forward. And you'll encounter some wonderful surprises about yourself, your ability, and your future.

PictoGame—Round 3

Let's take a look at the symbol for innovation, our windsurfer, and see what trouble he can get into with some pictograms. As with the previous Pathways, you'll find five situations illustrated on this page. See if you can identify at least one failed technique or a common barrier to innovation in each case. Then look over my answers at the back of the book. Don't get upset if your answers don't always agree with mine. Nobody said writing a book qualified me as a graphic artist!

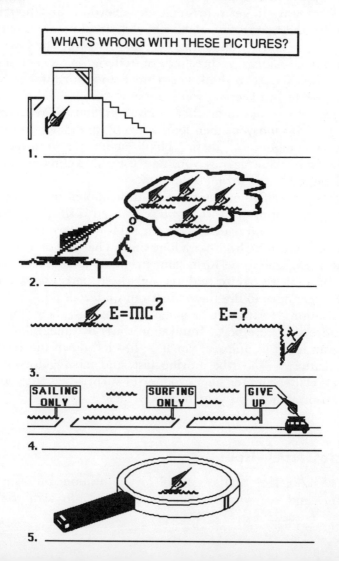

WHAT'S WRONG WITH THESE PICTURES?

1. _____

2. _____

$E = mc^2$ $E = ?$

3. _____

SAILING ONLY   SURFING ONLY   GIVE UP

4. _____

5. _____

4

Break
the Speed Limit

Losers react, winners respond.

The *Respond* Pathway

Bring Your New Ideas to Life _____

This chapter takes you across an important threshold. The first three Pathways dealt with creative solutions. The next three deal with courageous action. By listening, prospecting, and innovating, you synchronize your thoughts and plan your next moves according to the new rules, the rules being written by change. These next Pathways—Respond, Adapt, and Lead—put those thoughts and plans into motion. Here's where your new ideas come to life. The first three Pathways help you tune into the environment around you and the potential within you. The final three help you turn on power and turn up performance. If you can make it over this threshold from smart *observer* of today's events to successful *participant* in them, you'll *save yourself*. You'll start getting to the payoff. You begin by learning how to respond.

Losers React, Winners Respond

One of the highest compliments we can give an individual or an entire organization is that it's *responsive*. The worst is that it's *reactive*. The best way to come to grips with the Respond Pathway is to start with this distinction: Losers react, winners respond.

I want you to know exactly what *respond* means, to understand the critical difference between fast, targeted, successful responses and slow, clumsy, ineffective reactions. Everybody can react to change. Few have the sense and courage to respond. I'll show you how to respond, how to get things done quickly, with little effort, with minimum hassle, and how to get credit for them. You'll bypass others in the process, others who are wasting their time, energy, and, in fact, their lives in a futile struggle to win by the old rules. The ones who don't know the Pathway and who end up frustrated and defeated down some dumb dead end.

The Subtle Difference Between Winning and Losing

The dictionary tells us that to *respond* is "to show favorable reaction." The last three words hold the key—*show, favorable,* and *reaction*. Reaction is the expected result of any stimulus, and even a laboratory animal can react when it's poked or prodded enough. But unless your reaction to change is *favorable*, and *demonstrable*, it's not responsive. Reaction alone is not enough. And to react internally, or without showing your intention and concern to clients, customers, or the public, isn't responding.

And if you've done all the work and gotten little or none of the payoff for it, you haven't been responding. You've been taken.

If listening is the beginning of communication, responding is its highest form. Responding demonstrates interest, sincerity, concern, and dedication to results. It's not enough just to *be* interested, dedicated, and so on. You've got to *show* that you are and get paid for it. Responsive people and their organizations show a bias toward action, a willingness to try, and a commitment to results. The rest are slaves to work.

The Frustrated Frog and the Beauty of Closure

Look around and notice how many people are working without results. They're rushing back and forth, talking on the phone, writing memos and letters, going to meetings, laboring over plans, arguing, plotting, playing games, and creating a lot of confusion. Whether it's an office, factory, store, hospital, or school, you see a tremendous amount of effort. Much of it is just that: effort. Everybody is working, but unless you're in a supereffective place, little work is produced. That is, *work* is there, but it's a verb, not a noun. The completion, the final resolution, the *closure* of that effort is elusive.

Closure is the end, the net result, the payoff of effort. If we quit doing all the things that don't lead directly to closure, we'll have a lot less *working* (as a verb). And we'll get a lot more *work* (as a noun) done.

A long time ago I was puzzled by the story of the jumping frog. It seems if you put a frog on the floor ten feet from a feeding dish and with each jump it was able to clear half the distance between it and the dish, it would never make it to the dish. No matter how long you gave it, the frog would keep jumping closer and closer, and the distance between it and the dish would get shorter and shorter, but it would never get to it. Even given an infinite amount of time, it would go hungry. By definition it could only jump half the way, no matter how short that way became.

How an Inch Can Become a Million Miles

How many times have you felt like that jumping frog—when despite all your efforts, the problem never went away, closure never occurred? If you have failed to make it to your "feeding dish," you should know that *working more* never pays off. The problem has to be redefined. You've got to restructure the game. You can no longer accept the rules. Jumping halfway, three-quarters of the way, or 99 percent of the way doesn't get there, no matter how close you are or how many times you jump. The distance between *close* and *closure* might as well be a million miles.

People who don't understand the difference between response and reaction remind me of that jumping frog. They rarely reach closure. They keep looking up, as a frog would to its trainer, and expecting reward for their effort. But contemporary organizations, your place of work, no longer reward effort. They reward results. That's another way to define the Respond Pathway: a single-minded pursuit of results, regardless of how they come about, as long as they come about quickly and effectively.

How do you get results? How do you bypass the obstacles, blind alleys, and pitfalls and drive straight to the payoff? Start by using these *fast-forward* techniques.

Fast-Forward Responding

1. *Listening is responding.* Service-driven organizations know the power of listening. They know that simply to listen to people's concerns, objections, or suggestions is to respond. It is always favorable, and it always "shows." It's the difference between *selling* and *serving*. This is a dif-

ferent type of listening from that explained in Chapter 1. Here you're not intent on scooping in information. You're actually sending signals back to the source. You're *showing* that you're listening.

2. *Faster is better.*   Slow responses are no responses. The potential within a problem or an opportunity quickly plummets over time. Today's winners are those who can act quickly. Even if your specific response is not yet thought out or possible, start responding quickly. And let everyone else know it.

3. *It isn't until it's out.*   Customers never buy plans or intentions or analyses. They buy results. Success in responding is measured in terms of 0 percent or 100 percent. The frog doesn't get half his food when he jumps halfway to the dish. There is no partial credit. You may have a perfect idea, even a very innovative one, but it doesn't exist until you deliver it.

4. *Do it twice.*   Redundancy is no problem when it comes to satisfying someone else or meeting the needs of an organization. Respond verbally and in writing, send a representative and send a sample, write a procedure and give hands-on training. Since responding is the payoff, don't trust it to one method or to one attempt. A loop closed twice is better than an open one.

5. *Stop doing it.*   Make systematic corrections after or while isolated problems are being fixed. A common tendency is to fix symptoms or correct incidents. Fix the process that keeps creating them. Most solutions deal with the aftermath of troubles. We need to manage their "beforemath."

Listening on a "Need-to-Show" Basis

Most of us listen on a "need-to-know" basis. That's fine when you're listening to a recorded message, a CD player, or a radio. But when you're listening to a customer, a coworker, or any other real live person, I want you to start listening on a "need-to-*show* basis." That means your objective isn't necessarily to gain information, but to send signals back to the source—to show them you're hearing them, you care about what they're concerned with, and that you value what they have to say.

In my state we have a law requiring motorists to use their headlights in rain or fog, even in the daylight. A good number of drivers don't follow this because they're driving on a need-to-know, not -show, basis. They don't need the lights to see where they're going, so they don't turn them on. But you don't use your headlights in the rain or fog to see, you use them to be seen. They don't illuminate the road so you *know* where you're going, they illuminate you so you *show* where you're going—to others.

I wonder how many of us do the same at work, listening only when we need to listen—for us. And not listening well when we need to listen for them—for others. Visible, active listening is the easiest way to respond. You can tell when it's done and when it's not. You can see your boss when he or she is hearing you describe a terrific new idea or a terrible problem. Their eyes focus beyond you, their posture shows impatience, or they continually interrupt with put offs like, "I know, I know," or "Yes, yes, yes," or "Get to the bottom line, will you." They don't need your information and they signal they don't care. What they don't realize is how strong and negative that signal can be.

Sustain All Objections.   All of us have been mistreated at the grocery checkout, the rental car counter, or the local courthouse. We have a problem or a question, and the clerk won't even let it be heard before he or she barks out a "reaction." This is the worst way to solve an objection: refusing to allow the customer to object, refusing to hear him or her out.

Service-oriented people know that simply letting the customer ventilate an objection reduces the heat and pressure that it generates. When someone rushes up to you all agitated or excited, let them know you share that concern or excitement. Let them know you want to learn more about it. Give them space and time to get it out. Listen and let them know you're listening. Nine times out of ten that's all you have to do. They've gotten it off their chests, enlisted a friend or helper, and feel 100 percent better. Never keep an objector from objecting. Never signal that they haven't the right to object or that you haven't the time to listen to it. Take notes, ask them to repeat it again, slowly. Ask questions. Then review it with them. "Let's make sure I've gotten this all down," you should say, or "Do you mean that every one of your rental car's tires was flat?"

You might have been the person who slashed the guy's tires. It doesn't matter. You've got to show concern and allow the steam to escape. When someone is upset, angry, or excited, they're carrying a big load on their shoulders. Listening lets them transfer it to you. What's great is that they lose a ton and you gain an ounce. Take it. Don't try to keep it on them, even if they deserve it.

At the Happy Hotel.   A while back I was on a lecture tour and checked into a posh hotel in Madison, Wisconsin. I had been traveling and speaking all day, was pretty tired, and showed up at the hotel around 7:00 p.m. Since I had booked reservations in advance, I had no trouble checking in. I unlocked the door and set my luggage down in the dark, closing and locking the door behind me. After fumbling around a minute, I flipped the light switch and looked into my room to find, to my great surprise, a man and a woman making furious love on the bed!

Needless to say, I beat a hasty retreat out of there! When I reported this problem to the desk clerk, he asked me with a smile if I wanted to keep the room or would I prefer another! I was mad as hell. This guy was being flippant at a time when I was tired, upset, and seriously considering what would have happened had one of the two bedmates been within reach of a firearm!

His mistake was in not allowing me to be mad, not sharing my concern. All he had to do was listen. He preferred to crack a joke. The president of the hotel chain didn't laugh. After an exchange of correspondence, he fired the guy. I think he was last seen playing piano in a bordello.

Faster Is Better

This should be the motto of every person and every business. The pace and intensity of our world reward those who can get it done and get it done quickly. And we should all know that *a slow response is no response*. Whether we're talking about fixing a problem or exploiting an opportunity, the turtle only wins the race in fairy tales. In Turmoil it gets atomized.

There are two reasons that speed is so essential to all of us. The first has to do with competition. There is simply more of it nowadays. The slower you are in meeting a need, any need, the more you open the door for others to meet it before you can. And there are a lot of others out there waiting for that door to open.

But individuals compete as well. If you solve the problem first, your job competitors lose. If you mull it over, think about it for a while, put it on the back burner until it absolutely, positively has to get done, someone will beat you to the punch. You might have a better solution, a cheaper one, a more sensible one. But if they get to results before you, you have no solution at all. Get it done fast.

Living at the Speed of Light. The second reason for an increased premium on speed has to do with today's lifestyles. We're getting pretty used to instantaneous service today, and anything less is a loser. We live at the speed of light: pushing a few buttons on our phones and talking to someone in London, pushing a cassette in our car player and getting music, pushing a key on a word processor and getting immediate printouts. Waiting is not programmed into much of what we do. Neither is it part of human nature to wait. Patience does not come naturally. Remember childhood?

The people you deal with every day come from this world. They get their lunches in three minutes at McDonald's, they get their doctor's visits in ten minutes at a roadside medical center, they get their photos back in an hour. They get their microwave food in a flash. They get extremely frustrated when they push your button and get a "please hold" reaction. In the game of Turmoil, nobody waits anymore. Time is of the essence.

It's not that you've got to operate at the speed of light or that you've got to compete with computers or robots. Here's the secret to fast response: You don't have to reach closure in a nanosecond—just signal that your disk drives are spinning, that you're actively going after the result. Send that signal early; you'll give yourself plenty of time to act on it. Tell them that you felt your button being pushed, that you "heard" their request.

How to Keep From Getting Kicked.   What does this mean in practical terms? It means that when your boss asks you to look into a complex problem, one that will take three months to study, you send her a plan or an interim report in two days. It means that when someone asks you to get back to them in a week, you call them before the week is out, even when you have nothing to say. Silence is deadly here. Tell them you have nothing to say but just wanted them to know you're working on it.

I'm not suggesting you try to compete with electronic machines at response time. I'm suggesting you're dealing with people who get served by machines dozens of times a day, instantaneously, and are therefore less and less patient than previous generations. If you want to be treated like a machine, don't respond at all. That's the lesson of the Coke machine. When a Coke machine is out of drinks, and its sold-out light doesn't work, it gobbles coins and gets kicked, over and over. Studies show that machines that signal they're empty receive no such kicks. That's what's important: signaling back—at the speed of light.

Shifting From Tasks to Responsibilities.   An inescapable phenomenon is taking place all over the business world, including the place where you work. It's simple, but the impacts are revolutionary. *Work is being transformed from a series of steps or tasks to a bundle of responsibilities for results.*

People used to be divided into specialty groups or classifications and told to do one activity over and over, like on an assembly line. Management broke the work into small, simple steps, assigned these steps to others, then set up a process whereby the steps linked together to produce a product or a service. One person put on tires, one put in the windshield, one installed the steering column, and at the end of the line a car popped out. Or a customer placed an order with a sales representative, he or she delivered it to the order-entry clerk, who passed a requisition along to the stock clerk, who pushed a box over to the shipping clerk, who called the trucker, who delivered the box to the customer. Work was a closely linked series of dominoes, each touching the next one. Each domino knew exactly what to do and when to do it. They also knew what they weren't supposed to do—what was some other domino's job. Organization charts depicted this arrangement, and people were shown in a neat, stacked set of boxes that formed a pyramid. Executives on top, middle management in the middle, workers on the bottom floor. No more. The dominoes aren't touching and the pyramids are crashing down.

You're Getting More Freedom and Less Protection.   Work can no longer be divided into discrete steps, and people can no longer be chained to them. Our world of work is getting too complex, cumbersome, and unreliable. Modern entrepreneurial organizations are flat, with wide-ranging responsibilities assigned to flexible groups, not tall, with narrow sets of tasks assigned to focused individuals. In the past few years, they have taught the big corporations, the huge organizations, how to do it. It works and it is the model for the future. Most organizations are in the middle of this change. I mention it here because it affects you, not only what you do and how you relate to others, but what and how you think. You've got to change in all these areas in order to come to grips with our changing world.

The first lesson is this: All of us are being given fewer orders, fewer instructions, fewer details, and more responsibility. Rather than a list of dos and don'ts, we're given objectives, guidelines, visions, and "cultures." The time when we could point to the domino on the right or left of us and say, "She's supposed to do that," is drawing to a close. The time when we could say, "I did what I was supposed to, I don't know where it went after that," is over. Contrary to what some people may think, this universal change in the way work is done gives us more freedom, more flexibility, and more discretion. But it also means we have less protection from failure—that we can't hide behind procedures, job descriptions, pay classifications, or job titles. We win or lose with results.

It Isn't Until It's Out

When the legal brief isn't done on time, we can't say, "I gave it to Deborah to type yesterday." When the product blows up in the customer's face, we can't say, "I built it exactly as the specifications required." When the proposal is late in the client's office, we can't say, "But I sent it to the mailroom on Monday. They must have lost it."

Here's the point...like it or not: You and I get paid, promoted, and otherwise rewarded for getting work done, not for doing work. We take the credit when it's done and the heat when it's not. Are you going to trust your paycheck, your job, or your sanity to some guy in the mailroom, to the specifications someone else wrote, or to the typist? Are you going to trust that the dominoes will fall exactly as they're supposed to? Not me. I'm out to save myself. Here's how to respond to this new load of responsibilities.

1. *Don't ever assume.*   Murphy's Law is more active in times of change and when time is tight.

2. *Check, follow up, and follow through.*   You don't win when you've done your job. You win when the job is done.

3. *It's not out when it leaves your desk, your office, or your computer.*   It's out when it's out. And it doesn't do anybody any good when it's half out, three-quarters out, or 99 percent out. It's either out or it's not. It's either done or it's not. No partial credit in Turmoil.

The Responsibility Grenade.   If I had one piece of advice to give you in this chapter, this is it: *You are becoming more and more accountable for results, no matter what your job description, contract, or procedures say.* Failure at work is like a grenade: When it explodes, everybody gets hit. You can argue whether it's fair, whether you've been given the authority to go along with the added responsibility, and whether everybody else is holding up their end. But if you really want to *save yourself*, if you want to escape criticism and receive tribute, make sure you go for closure on *everything* you're associated with.

Do It Twice

Do things always go as they should? Is everybody smart, hard-working, and careful? Are others conscientious, concerned, and competent—all of them? Is everybody happy and excited about work? Does the secretary, assistant, mail carrier, shipping clerk, trucker, subcontractor, temporary, and new hire want *you* to succeed as much as you do? Do airplanes take off and land on time? Does everyone remember to do what they're supposed to do? Are you living in Fantasyland? Of course not. Now you know why redundancy exists: to make sure things get done.

Redundancy has been a design principle on high-risk systems for years. Take the space program. Every vehicle has back-up systems, emergency spares, manual overrides, and the like. This isn't because the risk of failure in any one of these systems is high; it's usually low. It's because even a small risk is unacceptable when millions of dollars and several lives are at stake. The extra cost and hassle of redundancy are worth it. They protect the result: a safe and effective mission.

Aren't you in a similar situation, facing risks and vulnerable to error, carelessness, laziness, and incompetence by others? When the results start to count more than the effort, redundancy starts to look pretty good.

Playing It Safe and Smart.   Two forces compel us to "do it twice," or choose redundant, even more expensive and less efficient ways to get things accomplished. First, we are so much more interdependent today. Few things can be done by one person who cares about the outcome and has control of every step in the process. Many more people are involved, increasing the chances for things to go wrong. Second, the rules and relationships among these people are constantly changing. None can be taken for granted or relied upon.

When things were pretty stable, when work was pretty straightforward and unchanging, you could learn how things worked and assume they would continue to work in that way. This is not only foolish today, but it's dangerous. People change jobs more frequently; procedures are constantly revised; companies are bought, merged, automated, and otherwise changed at a moment's notice. On top of that, most observers agree that a good number of workers—people upon whom you rely to get something done—are careless, unconcerned, and untrained. No one knows, moreover, how many are on drugs or alcohol, or are having severe personal problems (marital, gambling, whatever). Are you going to assume that everything will click into place—that things will work as they should as long as you do your job? Considering all of this, I can think of no better way to place yourself in jeopardy. If you want to *save yourself*, you've got to resort to redundancy, to back-up systems, to doing it twice, even though in Fantasyland you should only have to do it once. Turmoil is the game here, not trust.

Losers Have Hope, Faith, and Trust—Winners Have Results. What does this mean in everyday activity? It means that sending a letter doesn't constitute closure. Send a letter and follow up with a phone call. It means telling someone to be at 5th Avenue and 122d Street won't work. You've got to tell them the address and then tell them, "It's the red brick building across from the service station. It's two stories high with a green and white WAREHOUSE sign on top." Give more information than the minimum. Give the same information two different ways. Tell two people so one can remind the other. If you want it done right, do it twice.

When you send a voicemail message, ask for confirmation. When you send something Federal Express, make sure the person you give it to knows the difference between Federal Express and UPS. When you conclude a meeting, make sure each person repeats what their assignments are. Don't leave anything to chance, tradition, trust, faith, or hope. Results count. The work you performed, the hoops you jumped through, the safety precautions and redundancies don't. When it's all done, these evaporate. Only the success or failure of the effort remains. There is no partial credit in Turmoil.

When to Get Nervous. Here's a final note on this technique. Get very nervous whenever you hear anything that remotely resembles the following statements:

1. *But we always....* (Nothing is always.)
2. *Our procedure is...* (Procedures are made to be broken.)
3. *We never have any problems with...* (There's always a first time.)

4. *That's impossible...* (Everything's possible, especially failure.)

5. *Trust me,...* (Your response should be, "Show me.")

Customers don't pay when the shipping order is complete. They pay when the goods are in their hands. Presentations don't get made when the artwork is sent to the slide makers. They get made when the visuals are on the screen. Contracts aren't signed when the rough drafts are sent to word processing. They're signed when the ink goes on the paper.

If it seems like I'm overemphasizing this point, it's true. I am. Perhaps I'm following my own advice, doing it twice. But that's a small price to pay for getting it done. Considering the emphasis on results, the new culture of accountability, and the risks of change and complex interdependencies we face today, redundancy is a virtue and not a vice. *No one gets ahead by doing work. They get ahead by getting work done.* If you understand this subtle yet critical distinction, and if you put this advice into practice, you'll be saving yourself daily.

Stop Doing It

The common reason things aren't done is that other things are done instead. Everybody has more work than the time to do it, more priorities than ever before, and more pressure to meet them than in the past. This technique isn't about making to-do lists or prioritizing the tasks you're always wrestling with. It's much more blunt: *Stop doing much of what you're doing. Quit it.* If you're like most people, half of it is wasted effort, not leading to results. Or it's causing more effort, more problems, more delay.

Look at every pesky, troublesome activity and ask yourself if it's worth the bother. What does it lead to? Does it absolutely have to be done? Can it be done by someone else, sometime else, in some other, easier way? And finally, give it the supreme test: Who would know or care if it wasn't done at all?

Ripping Off the Band-Aids.   Here's where my earlier reference to *courageous action* hits home. To realize the entire potential of these Pathways, you've got not only to think differently but to act differently. And what better way to start than to question and abandon some of the useless, nice-to-have-but-not-results-critical work that's probably gobbling up a good portion of your time and energy? It's a fact that most people can add work, but only a few have the nerve and conviction to subtract it. It's easy to add someone to the distribution list, to invite someone else to a meeting, to send a copy to another person, to insert a contract clause, or to adapt another inspection step. But who's got the courage to do the opposite: to delete, omit, bypass, or remove? Procedures, instructions, and policies are like sticky balls rolling through the workplace: They pick up everything in their paths and end up huge, cluttered, and overpowering. This is the result of the Band-Aid phenomenon: It's easier to stick one on than tear one off. Start tearing them off everywhere they're not needed to stop bleeding. Most will never be missed.

Don't Do What You Can, Do What You Want or Need.   Be ruthless about this. Question why things are done, and if there is no answer that satisfies you, stop doing them. If a meeting is called, ask if it can be handled over the phone or if you have to be there. If a report is sent to someone, ask if he or she needs it. One of the hidden dangers of our electronic age is that we now have the capability to do many things that need not be done. Because a computer program can spew out spreadsheets any way from Sunday doesn't mean we need them, should send them, or must read them. Because a voicemail system can send a message to a hundred people at the touch of a button doesn't mean they need to listen to it. Because an airplane flies there doesn't mean you have to be on it.

Ben Franklin said it this way, "Just because one *has the right to do something* doesn't mean it's best to be done." We can rephrase this wisdom today as, "Just because we *have the capability to do something* doesn't mean we should do it." Dump everything you can that doesn't lead to results. Then increase the effort on what remains. The results will start to roll in, they'll be positive, and they'll show. You'll be responding, not reacting.

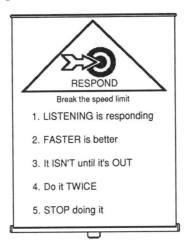

RESPOND
Break the speed limit

1. LISTENING is responding

2. FASTER is better

3. It ISN'T until it's OUT

4. Do it TWICE

5. STOP doing it

Barriers to Breaking the Speed Limit

Even the best-informed, best-intentioned among us fail to respond favorably and quickly to opportunities and problems. They might find Pathways to sudden excellence, but they don't take them. This isn't because they don't want to improve or innovate. It's because of barriers in their way. Or it's because they consider reaction the same as response.

Common reactions that stop favorable responses are: denying the problem exists, making light of the opportunity, finding someone to blame, and "killing the messenger" who brings the problem to light.

Obvious barriers to responding include inertia, fear, and cumbersome processes or procedures. These delay or retard swift action. But there are some not-so-obvious barriers as well. It pays to know what they are so we can unlearn them, disregard them, design them out of our work, or go around them when we can't do otherwise.

1. It Isn't My Job. Problems and solutions aren't neatly packaged so they can be handled by one person, one department, or one division. It often takes combined effort, coordinated activity, and shared responsibility. If we look at our jobs narrowly, no one is "able to respond" (response-able). Today's jobs are more broadly defined, more loaded with responsibility, and more dependent on others. It's a double whammy: You've got more responsibility while the actual work is spread among more loosely linked people and more independent organizations. Accountability goes up; control over events goes down. This is why speed, redundancy, and dumping noncritical tasks are key: Faster is better, do it twice, and stop doing it.

2. The Quest for the "Easy No." A lot of people spend their workdays looking for the "easy no." This is how they avoid work, miss great opportunities, and lose out on new ventures. They approach every potential, every suggestion for improvement, and every chance to serve a customer with this need in mind: Where can I find the easy no? What's there about this that will stop it, slow it down, or make it go away? Is it one of these favorites?

- We've never done it before (or that way).
- That will require some more data (or a study or a committee or a task force).
- We're concentrating on something else this fiscal year.
- You didn't go through proper channels.
- We'd need to have a meeting on that.
- We don't have that scheduled (or budgeted or targeted or visioned or prioritized).
- You'll have to talk to _____ about that (anybody but me).

- That's against our culture (a relatively new entry).
- Let's address that after we're finished with _____ (insert latest crisis, buzzword, or fad).

Easy noes are everywhere. Anybody can find them. Some are so tired they're almost clichés. You know what they are before they're spoken. I remember the joke about the two men shipwrecked on a desert island. After many years, they had told each other the same jokes so many times they decided to use a shorthand method of recounting them. One guy would turn to the other and say "nineteen!" and the other would laugh. Then he'd say, "thirty-two!" and the first guy would roll on the sand holding his sides. I think we should categorize the easy noes this way. You'd make a suggestion to save the company a million dollars and your boss would say "nineteen!," and you'd reply, "Yeah, I guess you're right. It isn't our job."

3. Domino Thinking. Fast responses require parallel action—concurrent efforts—but most of us are trained to think in series and to act consecutively. *Domino thinking* means *A* has to be complete before *B* can be started and so forth. Sort of like life is one big domino game, where the action can only follow one path, in one direction, according to one and only one predetermined sequence. You know you're listening to domino thinking when you hear such key phrases as: "the way it's done around here...," or "We can't do that until...," or "First we do this, then we do that." Dominoes react, smart people and successful companies respond. And responding demands shortcuts, bypasses, and more than one thing happening at the same time—*antidomino thinking*.

One of the most significant inventions in management has to do with this principle. It's called "critical path" planning and scheduling. It came about in the 1950s and 1960s and is used to plan huge endeavors—like the construction of an oil refinery, the building of a nuclear submarine, or the relocation of a corporate headquarters—endeavors that take a long time and involve many complex, interdependent actions. Consultants specialize in it, computer programs do it, and universities teach it. It can get complex, but you can use it every day. Basically, it involves taking apart a process, looking at the steps it requires, and unlinking all the steps that can be unlinked so they can be started early and not end up holding up the entire job.

The easiest way to say this is, "Does *A* have to be done before *B* and *B* before *C*? Or can *A* and *B* be done at the same time, and then *C*?" In other words, do these three things have to be done in series (end-to-end), or can they be done in parallel (overlapping)? You'd be surprised how many tasks are done one after the other that can be done much quicker in parallel. Bottlenecks can be eliminated, people's work loads can be smoothed, and delays can be avoided. Entire schedules can be compressed, saving all sorts of time.

The result isn't different, it's just achieved faster. Look at what you're doing, how each step is linked to another, and start breaking those links. Watch the time it takes to get things done start to shrink. When time shrinks, response grows. A turtle moves one foot at a time, one after the other. A rabbit has all four going simultaneously.

4. Aiming at Perfection. To respond at 95 percent is much better than failing to respond at 100 percent. The only perfect response is one that works and works within the limited time-window that we have to get it to work. Even if it takes much time and consideration, at least START and show others you have. People don't expect perfection, just a genuine and quick response.

Many of us are schooled differently. As accountants, we're taught to get it right, to balance the numbers no matter how long it takes. As engineers, we're told to search for the optimum solution—the most efficient design, not the fast one. But these rules were written for the horse-and-buggy days, not for our laser-fast world. The careful, methodical, calculating response that gets there a day late is a recipe for disaster, but if it's a dollar short it's no big deal. Today's lessons shouldn't come from professors of accountancy or engineering, but from the pizza delivery boy: Get it there in thirty minutes or you don't get paid.

5. Loving Processes, Forgetting Results. This is similar to loving product features and forgetting their benefits, which was covered under the Innovate Pathway. Remember the cardinal rule that's been woven throughout this chapter: The benefit of a response is its results, not the activity leading to them. Don't get infatuated with the process that "normally" works—drive for results, for what will work now.

1. It isn't MY JOB

2. REASONS not to

3. DOMINO thinking

4. Aiming at PERFECTION

5. Loving PROCESSES, forgetting RESULTS

Efficiency Is Out, Effectiveness Is In

Here's the crux of another revolution sweeping businesses around the world. *Effectiveness is now more important than efficiency.* It's the same distinction as that between *work* as a verb and *work* as a noun. Effectiveness means leading to expected results. Efficiency means smooth operations. People don't get excited about a smooth-running operation that produces the wrong results or late results. In the battle of Turmoil, your ray gun might not be the most efficient. But if it's effective, if it stops the invading alien from eating you, it's the greatest ray gun on earth!

When I was in graduate school studying business logistics, we were taught that air freight was the most inefficient way to ship bulk materials or heavy items. Better to consider river barges or railroads if you must. This makes sense if you're shipping coal, oats, or cement. You wouldn't want to ship an entire automobile by air either. That's inefficient. But when the President of the United States flies to California to make a speech, his back-up plane carries an armored limousine. Why? It's effective. It's there when he needs it. Do you want to be the one who tells him, "Sorry, Mr. President, but your limo is on a barge somewhere in the Ohio River. Why don't you take the bus to the convention center. It's more efficient?"

Breaking the Bank

As we saw with the Innovate Pathway, no features are more important than the benefit they bring, no matter how efficient, neat, or high-tech they may be. And it doesn't help to do things right if you do the wrong things. I remember working for a large bank in Melbourne, Australia. I was recommending a reorganization at the same time another American consultant happened to be reviewing their security systems, particularly the protection of their national data center. Where banks used to build vaults to hold gold or cash and protect them with every precaution, they now guard an even greater treasure: their computers. You can steal their cash and rob their customers, but if you mess with their files, their data, their information systems, you're really hurting them.

The security consultant was being briefed by the bank's director of security, a man obviously proud of his precautions. He was showing the consultant the door to the data center, one studded with locks and alarms, and under constant camera surveillance. Pointing to the elaborate devices, hidden mechanisms, and carefully designed measures, he said, "No one has yet to beat this system, not even the security experts who designed it. It's the best in the nation, absolutely fool-proof. No worries, mate!" I watched as the consultant studied the heavily protected door for a moment. He then took a set of rental car keys from his pocket, pried up the hinge nails on the special door, and removed it, opening the data center for all to see. He explained to his astonished host that thieves just want to get in. They don't really care about how intricate the system may be. Seems the bank had been so concerned with locking the door, strengthening, and alarming it, that they installed the hinges inside out! They fell in love with their wonderful security features and ignored their purpose. No system exists to impress consultants or to reassure security officers. It exists to keep thieves out. This one was *all effort, no effect.*

More Proaction Tips and Tricks

Because the ability to respond is now the same as the ability to survive, I've got a few more tips and tricks for you to consider.

Eliminate the endless loop.

Computer programmers and planners use the term "endless loop" to mean an activity that can't come to an end, a sort of lobster trap where you can get in (start) but can't get out (end). How does this work in everyday business? Suppose you embark on a program to pursue "excellence." How do you know when to stop? How do you stop trying to be excellent? I can just hear you addressing the troops: "Okay, everybody, as of 9:00 a.m. we've achieved excellence, so we don't have to improve anymore." Instead, pick a target that you can hit, a *measurable* achievement. A result that squeaks when it's met.

Be there at the finish.

All politicians know this. Why else would they appear at a ribbon-cutting ceremony even though they opposed funding for the project? If you've done most of the work, be there for the credit. It might be merely ceremonial, and you might have better things to do. Don't think that matters. In times of turmoil, he or she who's there at the finish gets credit for the closure.

Finish first and set the standard.

We all remember this from high school. Some smarty hands in his or her term paper a week ahead of time, and the teacher expects everyone else's to be as long, neat, and comprehensive as that first one. The rule hasn't changed: The first one done sets the standard for everyone who follows. Be the one who sets the standard, not the one who has to meet it. Rush to closure.

Make "yes" easy.

Remember how many are out there looking for the easy no? Don't let them get it, especially when you want a sale made, a contract signed, a concession granted, or an idea approved. Think through the easy noes before you present your case. Determine why each is unacceptable. Present your case for your idea and your case against the easy noes at the same time. Don't give the other party a nanosecond to grab an easy no before you destroy or discount it. An easy no is like an escape hatch for someone who wants to avoid you or your idea. Lock the hatches, or put alligators on the other side.

Get obsessed with service.

If *excellence* was the business buzzword of last decade, *service* is its contemporary replacement. Everybody is looking for better service, bragging about their service, attending service seminars, and reading service books. Cloak your ideas and responses in this notion of service. This isn't just a cute trick. *The idea of service is at the heart of the Respond Pathway.* Service is the intersection of need and fulfillment, the point where what you have done crosses what other people want done. Notice I use the phrase "have done" and not "are doing" or "are going to do." Service is very time-dependent. It's instantaneous, occurring precisely and only at the moment it's felt by the one being served.

Responding = Service

Service is in the eyes of the receivers, of the ones served. And their views on service differ depending on their psychological makeup, expectations, and customs. I might be wrong, but I'll give you some specific advice here. What turns on a twenty-year-old does little for someone in their golden years, and vice versa. I think the nature of a good response (and therefore good service) is a factor of age and background. Let's look at three different groups.

1. *The elderly or senior citizens.* Most were born during the depression or shortly thereafter. Because of this, they treasure security and stability, and they feel that social position has been earned and therefore is important. Treat them accordingly. If you're in the service business (most of us are), show them security, respect, and stability.

2. *The baby boomers.* It's a different story here. This group was herded into crowded schoolrooms and crowded through the military and other social institutions. They've always been in a crowd, put in alphabetical order—treated like numbers and not like individuals. If you want to serve them, emphasize individuality and distinctive features. They want their space, the ability to step away from the crowd. They don't want what everybody gets, they want it their way. Freedom and individuality are their hot buttons.

3. *The trailers, the ones born after the baby boom.* This

group is smaller, had smaller classes at school, didn't go through the regimentation and conformity of the military, and had more individual attention from parents, teachers, and authority figures. They expect personal attention. They expect to be asked how they're doing, how their meal tastes, how they enjoyed the play, and how comfortable their airplane seat feels. Many were brought up in blended families, with single parents, or in impersonal day-care centers and the like. They like you to address them by name and show personal, individual interest in their comfort.

Moving On

What you've found in this chapter is a collection of ways to get more work done by working less. Many of them aren't new, and some of them are commonsense explanations of complex process design principles used by management consultants worth their salt. But what's new is the emphasis on speed, effectiveness, interdependency, and risk: the new wrinkles brought on by our constantly changing circumstances.

The new rules of results have deposed the old rules of conduct. Some of the old rules have to be unlearned, and some sacred cows have to be shot. Most of the anxiety and pain felt by today's workers is due to this transition: We're working in the new world, under the new pressures, and yet we're still laboring under the old rules and the outmoded assumptions...or our bosses are. It will take many, many years for this discrepancy to be rectified, for the new working methods and the new mindsets to catch up to the new working conditions. For the meantime, we're stuck in the middle. Anything you can do to see the new rules, put them into play, and bypass the ones that don't work anymore will help you survive.

As you can tell, most of the techniques and barriers are described fairly dramatically, as if the old way was wrong and the exact opposite should be done. My intention is to emphasize the critical difference that even small distinctions can make, like the ones between *activity* and *accomplishment*, *efficiency* and *effectiveness*, and *series* and *parallel* work steps. My experience tells me that these seemingly minor distinctions, these subtle differences, are much more than we give them credit for. They are actually the difference between being fulfilled and being frustrated. They are the difference between working and winning, between finding a place and a career and falling through the cracks, and finally, between reaping the rewards that are out there or getting replaced.

Next Stop—Magic!

As you start using these techniques, you'll find you're not only changing the work that you do and how you do it, you'll be changing the way you think about work. You'll be changing yourself. I hope this happens because I know that only by constantly changing can you expect to stay ahead of the change curve. That's the next challenge for you: learning how to adapt to new conditions quickly, to use new techniques, and to see yourself in a new way. It's time to enter the Adapt Pathway, to learn more about the magic of our era: *change*.

PictoGame—Round 4

Now it's time to practice your imagination once again, only this time using the on-target symbol for the Response Pathway. As the pictograms on the following page show, the arrows just aren't getting to the target. Something is wrong in each case. Make your best guess as to what that might be, then flip to the answers at the back to see what I found.

WHAT'S WRONG WITH THESE PICTURES?

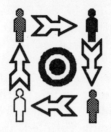

1. _____

2. _____

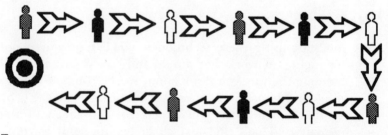

3. _____

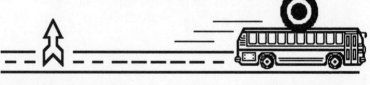

4. _____

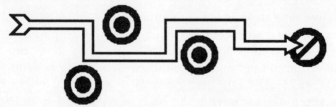

5. _____

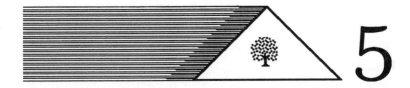

5

Break Into
the Future

The future belongs to the adaptive.

The *Adapt* Pathway

Change Yourself to Save Yourself

To *adapt* means to make fit for a new use or situation, often by modification. To reach the promise of this Pathway, you've got to examine yourself, critically, and have the courage to abandon or modify what isn't working anymore. In other words, you've got to change. If only it were that simple and that easy.

Every one of us has a love/hate relationship with the concept of change. I want to help you turn down the hate and turn up the love. This is because, like it or not, change is now synonymous with survival. The message is becoming quite clear: *Change or die.* Most of us know this by now. Most of us know that change is no longer an option but a prerequisite to

survival and sanity. There is a great difference, however, between knowing that change is mandatory and knowing *how
to change*. Follow me down the Adapt Pathway, and I'll show
you how it's done.

Changing by Design, not by Default

The world is full of people and companies swept up by the
forces of change. Most have little choice: Change is forced on
them, and they drift along with no control and no idea of
where it's taking them. These are the ones *changing by default*. I'm not interested in that type of change, nor should
you be. I'm interested in *changing by design*, having some say
in where change is taking me, and being able to capitalize on
it. The Adapt Pathway isn't a prescription for acceptance, for
being slam-dunked by change and learning to like it. It's a
process of controlling change—of knowing when, where, and
how to manage your way through the phenomenon. I want
you to take this perspective, to make change a process of
choice, not chance.

No Warm and Fuzzy—No Soft and Squishy

I won't be asking you to contemplate the dynamic universe,
reevaluate your lifestyle, or alter your personal makeup. I'll
not leave you with a seminar-thin veneer of knowledge about
the meaning of change, nor will I make it into a warm and
fuzzy, cotton-candy topic: all fluff and no stuff. Change is
tough as hell. It causes pain, frustration, and anxiety. It usually hurts. But it can't be avoided. The question isn't whether
you *will* change. You *must* change. The question is whether
you'll *win through change*, whether you'll have a stake in the
future, a part in its design and a share of its promises.
Whether you'll change by design or by default. Whether
you'll pull yourself into the future or be pushed out of it.

There isn't a third alternative: You either buy a ticket to the future or you accept a sentence to the past. The concept of a comfortable present is now fiction.

Change is like a river: You're either swimming with the current or against it. You can never stop the current, especially today, when the current is overpowering. Only the adaptive can cope with it.

Each of the previous Pathways leads you to change. Listening helps you pick up on its signals. Prospecting and Innovating help you change your understanding and your approach to problems and opportunities. Responding directs change, puts it to work, makes it bring results. With the Adapt Pathway, you'll change your chances at change. You'll become not only *changed*, tuned into today's world and actively engaged with it, but *changeable*—ready to retune and reengage.

Our Love/Hate Relationship With Change

Every human being has a love/hate relationship with this vague thing we call change. We hate change because it threatens our stability and comfort. We love it because it brings exciting challenges and promising prospects. We hate the way it upsets settled habits, but we love the break in boredom it brings. We hate having to accept new ways of working but look forward to gaining new skills and a renewed sense of mastery. Change disturbs established relationships among us, but it creates new ones in its wake. We hate it because it *forces* us to learn yet love it because it *lets* us learn. And we hate change that breaks what's fixed but love it when it fixes what's broken.

Prescription for a World on Fire

The only other phenomenon I can compare to change is *fire*. We hate fire that burns down a forest but love it when it keeps us from freezing to death. Fire extinguishes lives but lights up the darkness. It powers our machines and fuels our nightmares. Fire and change—both powerful, both dangerous and vital—friends when under control, deadly when not.

Learning to change doesn't mean blindly accepting all changes and going along with everything that's new or different. It's respecting the power of change, understanding how it acts and putting that knowledge to work in a proactive way. It's taming and domesticating change, much as our ancestors learned to harness and control fire. Changes occurring today can't be approached along this old love/hate angle. They're too involved to hate or love, and your reaction shouldn't be that simple. Indeed, one of the most serious errors would be to embrace all changes indiscriminately. I'll show you why this is dangerous, too, like embracing all fire. As with fire, change should be treated with caution. Otherwise you'll embrace it so closely you'll turn yourself into a torch.

The Executive Turnaround

In the late 1970s I began to explore this curious phenomenon in earnest. Since then I've written books on it, lectured on it, and helped scores of organizations around the world as they tried to understand it and control it. In the early days, corporate executives defended the status quo as they would their stock options: They fought change with a passion. They questioned me, the concept, and the necessity of change. "Change?" they'd say. "We're too good (or big, or small, or special, or poor, or rich, or successful, or fragile)." I found few sympathetic ears. I would come home from a consulting engagement or a lecture tour and wonder if I was the only one who considered change the phenomenon of our time. I felt like a voice in the wilderness, and a steadily weakening voice at that. "Great concept," they'd say, "but we think we'll pass on it."

Change or Die! _____

This all changed abruptly in the mid-1980s. Suddenly every executive, every board of directors, and every organization caught the fever. Change was now "in." It was as if American and European businesses all got the same wake-up call at the same time! I'm not sure, but I think that call was coming from the East—the Far East.

A number of factors contributed. Takeovers, mergers, acquisitions, downsizing, recapitalization, restructuring, tax law changes, deregulation of major industries, and above all—*exploding technology*, particularly information technology. We saw the convergence of a dozen factors, each pushing change, with the combined effect of a fire alarm in a crowded theatre. My phone started to ring and my frequent flier points started to mount quickly. It was time to hit the road. It was time to start talking and doing change.

Things are a bit different now. When I go to a corporation in the throes of change, I no longer hear "Why should we?"; I hear "How can we?" Organizations started to learn how to change, governments changed, and even the most traditional, reactionary managements and institutions on the face of the earth started to read the writing on the wall: *Change or die!*

The Attack of the Change Drivers _____

I used to advise executives to become *change drivers* (the causers of change) and got about the same reaction as if I'd asked them to become terrorists. Now there is rarely a member of top management who doesn't proudly proclaim to be a "change master." The message got through. But it took scores of bankruptcies, layoffs, losses of markets, and in the political arena, hundreds of thousands of people in the streets with banners and sometimes guns.

The result is that today most top managements, with some exceptions, are playing with change and learning how it's done. They're learning for better or worse how to stay even with or ahead of the change curve. It's time for the people who work in those companies to learn too. It's time *you* learned the tricks they're learning and put the fire of change to use for yourself.

This chapter will detail ways you can change and stay agile and ready for more change. I'll point out how you can survive change that is dumped on you from above (or below, or from the side) and how to start change yourself. Here's the program at a glance:

- Accept the law of change (change or die).
- Learn and practice the art of changing (fast-forward techniques).
- Escape the past, unlock the future (get past the barriers).
- Learn which end of the "change torch" to hold.
- Make change your ally; keep it from being your enemy.

Don't think that change is so new or so foreign. If you're an average citizen, statistics say you're already a change master, especially in your personal life. They say that in your lifetime you'll have three separate careers (not jobs, careers), one and a half marriages, make seven household moves, and own nineteen cars! If you can survive all that, adapting to business change will be a snap!

Change Forces You Should Know About

In other books, I've written of changes that are impacting organizations and how they should adapt to them, about organizational change. I won't repeat those causes or recommendations here. Instead, I'd like to get to the effects change has on *you*, the individual trying to cope in new, often uncertain conditions. What does change mean for you? Let's explore four major trends, changes that I see everywhere and that are bound to affect you.

Smaller Work Units With Shorter Life Spans. This trend exists from the smallest entrepreneurial start-ups to the megacorporations. Gone are the days when you could camp out in a particular department, division, or company, when you could find security or anonymity in a sea of desks in a large and stable organization. Organizations are now being shuffled like decks of cards at a poker convention, and new hands are dealt with greater frequency.

Not only are reorganizations, downsizing, and restructuring commonplace, but the very way people are assembled is changing. Small, focused teams are being created and aimed at singular problems or opportunities. When they complete their mission, they are disbanded and the members filter back into the mainstream or are reassigned to different and new teams. Whether they're called projects, task forces, teams, or autonomous self-managing work units, they are the wave of the future. Grab a bunch of people from all over, put them in a temporary group, give them a goal, and dissipate the group when the goal is achieved (or is missed, or the money runs out, or top management gets a new priority, or whatever).

What does this mean for you? To begin with, it means establishing relationships, learning processes, understanding others, and refocusing on new objectives continuously. It means a cycle of *learn, work, unlearn, forget*—over and over. This puts a new premium on the ability to adapt. It means "the way work is normally done" is an anachronism—a phrase from the past. Each work situation is different—different people, different positions, responsibilities, risks, goals, relationships, everything. There is little meaning to words like *normal, standard, traditional,* or *typical.* When these new groups are organizing and working together, "the way we did it last time" has about as much weight as a straw hat.

The up side of all this organizational turmoil is that it

opens new doors for aspiring leaders, a subject of the next Pathway: Lead. For if leadership can be defined, it's the ability to adapt and get others around you to adapt. This is the bright promise of organizational dynamics: No longer will you have to wait for a major reorganization or the retirement of others to move into a leadership vacuum. Change is creating these vacuums everywhere, all the time. In fact, you almost have to hug your desk to keep from getting sucked into one. If you want to win, this is terrific! If you want to hide or coast, this is scary.

Responsibility Is Flowing Down the Pyramid. The second major trend has been briefly mentioned already: *a downward flow of responsibility*. When the pioneers of what was then called "scientific management," Frederick W. Taylor and Frank Gilbreth, invented management in the 1920s, they presumed all responsibility would rest at the top. From an apex of control inhabited by an exalted executive, a pyramid of lesser and lesser managers would lead downward to supervisors, and finally, to the masses of workers. These workers would be told how to do everything (not why or what for—just how). They got their instructions on the most restricted "need-to-know" basis. They performed narrow, well-defined tasks (widgets on digits). Domino thinking was the only thinking going on. Responsibility and latitude were for the upper classes in the hierarchy: top management only.

Today this is being turned upside down. Responsibility, information, and accountability are flowing down the side of the pyramid like lava from a volcano. The function we call "managing" is also sliding downward, outward, and sideways. Everybody is given looser guidelines, more discretion, and less specific instructions. *Thought workers*, the so-called white-collar or information workers that make up the majority of today's companies, can be organized no other way.

The implications are clear: goal-oriented orders rather than specific procedures, and management-by-results (or by objectives) rather than by processes. Workers determine almost all of the *how* and even, in progressive companies, some of the *what*. This change of direction is made easier by the lightning speed and universal availability of data processing tools: computers. More can be known about how goals are being reached or missed by more people faster than ever before.

Some managements are trying to have it both ways: dumping responsibility downward and retaining authority at high levels. This is another feature of the present business landscape: people trying to manage with the old rules and the new ones simultaneously. It never works, and it sure causes those working under them tremendous grief. Regardless of this inequity, the trend of downward-flowing responsibility still exists. What it means is that you'll be forced to adapt to new goals more often, work with new people more frequently, and work in different ways. Constant adaptation is the key to surviving in this climate.

Working at Hyperspeed. These first two trends lead to a third: *the ever-quickening pace of business.* Change is accelerating work, compressing and reducing time, and intensifying immediate needs that demand almost instantaneous satisfaction. Competition is fanning this fire, and automation and information systems are fueling it. Real-time and "zero-wait state" aren't just terms for computer "tekkies." They're adjectives for today's business pace.

Leading management consultants used to point to the *learning curve* as a pattern for group work. According to this idea, groups of people or entire corporations started slowly at first, gained more experience with increased volume, and gradually increased their productivity and quality as more and more of the same type of work was performed. People settled into routines, mistakes were reduced, and relationships and rules of behavior were established. The big machine (group and group effort) might cough and sputter until its rpm's got high, but once it was in gear, it roared, cranking out more and more for less and less.

This is great theory, and it works when you've got thousands of repetitions, similar work tasks, fixed organizations, and constant conditions. All of which are now about as rare as slide rules, eight-track tape players, and '58 Edsels. We have compressed the learning curve so much that, in many cases, everything we do is being learned *while we do it*. The learning curve has been shortened to a *point*. Maybe a better term would be the "learning dot," or better yet, the "unlearning curve." And even if the work remained the same, the way we do it and the people who do it are constantly being revised, more reasons to learn how to adapt. We used to say, "Well, we made a few mistakes last time, but we'll do better next time." There is no "last time" anymore and no "next time." There's only one time for most efforts: this time— *now*.

Continuous Change, Forever. This final trend is also related to the *Now-ism* I mentioned in the Introduction: *Change doesn't quit, it just changes*. Companies can no longer change and then rest. They've got to be ready to change and change again, soon. After many of the so-called "excellent" companies cited in Peters and Waterman's seminal book, *In Search of Excellence*, started to crater, go belly-up, and otherwise crash and burn, executives finally realized that no one can get a lock on excellence. It's fleeting, and it demands constant renewal, continuous change. So expect change to be a lifelong challenge, no matter where you work. Too many forces are at work and too many competitors and alternatives are out there paying attention to them. No company, no person can call for a time out. The rules of Turmoil won't allow it. The future belongs to the adaptive.

The End of the Old Guard

I've been advising too many prehistoric thinkers to announce the end of outmoded management, at least at this point. But I am seeing it approaching its end. I'm seeing the ethos of executives change everywhere, from one which cherished *preserving* (the organization, the image, the assets, the market) to one where *provoking* (change, innovation, creativity, the competition) is in style. Sometimes this switch is in appearance only; executives embrace the buzzwords but not the implications. They still think in terms of a static, ordered world. Other times they are indeed firebrands. In either case, the first question most have when they make this mind switch, when they come up with a new proposal, strategy, or product is, "How can I get the rest of my organization to accept this change?"

Overcoming resistance to change is a key task in the process of adaptation. But I don't want to miss another important point. You need to do more than overcome resistance to change, more than accept change. I want you to use it, to master it, and to profit through it. I don't want you to be a change-acceptor but a change-initiator, a *change arsonist*. Set the place on fire, harness the energy of change, get behind it and get rewarded for it. And by all means, you don't want to get crushed by it.

How to Get Crushed by Change

Don't think that there aren't ways change can bite you, or burn you: There are. In this section I'll show five ways to be crushed by it. I'm not going to use any names or portray any past clients in a negative light. Let them be known by their actions. You'll recognize them everywhere. Just be careful not to see yourself as one of them.

1. *Be a martyr.*

The martyr fights for a cause that's not worth fighting for. He or she usually wants to protect an existing organization, whether it is a department, service line, or product team—to shield it from change at all costs. The martyr thinks the best way to stop a bonfire is to jump into it.

I was advising a large electric utility to centralize a certain design function among various projects. At the time, each of sixteen projects had one of these specialists, and the idea was to group them together so they could serve the entire company as required. In a meeting of the executive committee reviewing my recommendations was "Stan," the head of these specialists. He erupted in anger, objecting to every argument for consolidation and pointing out all sorts of reasons it wouldn't work. He made a martyr of himself. "My people want to be where they are. They can't work any other way!" he insisted.

Later I spoke with Stan alone. He'd been under extreme pressure to accept the consolidation and just couldn't see abandoning his loyal troops to its eventuality. He cited loss of esprit de corps, a decline in motivation, and the erosion of professional competence as certainties should the change go through.

He'd even gone to a doctor complaining of severe headaches, thinking he had a brain tumor. The doctor assured him it was stress. Stan was really getting bent out of shape on this issue. I suggested the sixteen loyal specialists be called to a special meeting with myself and Stan. Once he faltered through the proposal, almost losing his composure, I asked the group how they viewed the change. The results startled me. Eight had gotten wind of the consolidation and obtained transfers to other departments, including raises in pay for some. Six others thought it was a long-needed change and looked forward to it. Two relatively new employees said it didn't matter one way or the other! Here Stan, the martyr, had impaled himself in front of the top executives for a cause the troops didn't even buy. He didn't save himself. He sacrificed himself—for nothing!

2. *Get pigeonholed.*

If your father, mother, teacher, mentor, or coach ever told you to get very good at a narrow specialty so you'd always be rewarded, they steered you wrong. Becoming pigeonholed is a recipe for failure in changing times. You become associated with a product, project, function, discipline, or specialty that may be devalued, dumped, or disintegrated in the race to change. Always keep open, aware, and involved with other aspects of your company's operations. Do not become the company's best specialist in any field. Leave yourself the chance to change. If your name and a particular part of the work are synonymous, you're in trouble. If you can't move, shift, or jump, you can get run over. Companies diversify to protect themselves from the dynamics of the market. Take a tip from them: Diversify yourself.

3. *Be a whiner.*

This character can find nothing good about the future: everything sucks. Whiners might be right. The new idea might indeed suck, but even if it fails as predicted, no one will forget the whiner. No one gets credit after a change fails by saying, "I told you so!" They get hatred. Instead of whining, work with the change. Try to put your mark on it. Try to accept it and make the most of it. If you still can't stand it, get another job. Whining sucks.

4. *Appoint yourself the one who turns off the lights.*

This is the person who holds on to the very end, the last one to leave, the one who turns out the lights on the past when everyone else is enjoying the future. If a process, organizational structure, or particular way of doing things needs you as its guardian, it isn't very self-sustaining. Why should you tie your job, your sanity, and your future to something you didn't even know existed until you joined the outfit? Whoever waits until the "place" is empty becomes the last one to turn out the lights. And he or she ends up in the dark, alone. Not a smart way to survive.

5. *Become irreplaceable.*

One of the cruelest remarks you can hear is when someone is told they're replaceable. But being irreplaceable isn't so hot either. It means you can't move ahead because you're needed where you are. It means when what you do is replaced, you go out with it. It means tying yourself to a job, duty, or position that keeps you from adapting. The challenge of change is to be valuable and respected, but not irreplaceable. Even the president of General Motors wants to be replaced. He wants to move up to chairman.

Fast-Forward Adapting

Here are five techniques for those who want to know how to grow, to change, to adapt.

1. *Knock down walls.*   Dividing organizations into groups of specialists used to make sense, but the penalties are getting intolerable. "Walls" between two departments or divisions, between line and staff, or between one function and another lock the organization into rigidity. It's tough to preach teamwork when every group is out for itself. It's also next to impossible to get things done when isolated units either fear or misunderstand each other. Change doesn't respect internal structures. Neither should you.

2. *Unlearn.*   When you live in times of change, you not only have to change the way you work, but more importantly, you have to change the way you think. This is a new challenge, but a critical one. People can no longer assume that learning is additive—that you just keep stacking new lessons on top of old ones. Sometimes the old ones have to go. If you want to move with the times, you've got to have a garage sale of outdated habits and assumptions. Unlearning means creative forgetting—consciously questioning the rules and even the subconscious assumptions that just don't fit anymore.

3. *Turn enemies into friends.*   Changing times mean changing alliances. The "enemy" could become your new ally, and your former assistant could become your new boss. It

doesn't make sense to antagonize anyone or any company: The times are just too fluid. Companies that used to slug it out as competitors are suddenly merging. Suppliers who used to cheat customers are being bought by those very customers. The groups you fight with today may be your dancing partners tomorrow.

4. *Erase borders, grow people.*   Give everyone every opportunity to develop, to grow, to learn new skills, to master new challenges. When we could safely assume the work and the environment would be stable, we could classify people into slots, or into restrictive job definitions. Today's employee won't take this anymore. He or she wants growth, development. And for good reason. Change is the rule. If you're human, you probably have an imaginary border around most people's interests and talents, thinking they're a mechanic, a sales manager, an analyst, or whatever. If you want to adapt, you've got to erase these borders. Growth and change are synonymous.

5. *Raise the bar.*   This technique is at the center of adaptation—constantly setting higher and higher goals. The Japanese manufacturers who have been so successful program it into their processes. They just keep chasing higher and higher levels of quality, productivity, and market share. Why can't we, as individuals, do the same? Why can't we be blessed, rather than cursed, with persistent dissatisfaction? If necessity is the mother of invention, persistent dissatisfaction is its father.

Knock Down Walls

Walls are the structures of stagnation. They abound in rigid, nonresponsive organizations. They divide groups, stifle communication, and protect mediocrity. Most are functional, dividing groups of specialists from each other. Mobile, agile organizations can't shift with new opportunities when they're trapped behind walls.

Walls don't have to be made of stone or steel to keep people from adapting. I use the term to represent the boundaries between departments, divisions, and other organizational units. One trend is already knocking down these walls: the demise of the functional organization. This is the one where groups of specialists are arranged according to their skills or responsibilities, like with the accounting department, the finance department, the purchasing department, and so on. Today's organizations aren't a fixed collection of functional boxes as they were in the past. They're fluid, temporary "bubbles" of people assigned to unique and fleeting goals. Some functional arrangements still exist, a few for good reason but most out of simple tradition, and most are falling aside. The walls are tumbling down. Don't be the last one to see this.

Also keep in mind that the invisible perimeter that separates your organization or company from the outside world is coming apart. Companies aren't cell structures with impermeable boundaries. They're more porous today, with consultants, temporaries, joint-venture people, subsidiaries, contractors, and the like crossing the perimeters. Don't assume an unwarranted loyalty to the inside of the boundary, to "us" as opposed to "them." In a moment's notice, you could change from one to the other.

Bridging positions are ones that span the old boundaries, where you work between two or more groups, often in liaison or as a go-between. Look for these positions and get in one. You'll learn more, be more valuable, make more friends, and become more agile should change appear.

The Chauvinist Pigs of the Organization Chart. There are male chauvinists and national chauvinists, but there also are *group chauvinists*—people who see the company in terms of two camps. Everyone is classified as either "us" or "them." To group chauvinists, everything *we* do is right, and everything *they* do is wrong (or less efficient, or more stupid, or slower, and so on). Be careful not to let group loyalty get out of hand here. If you wear the uniform long enough, it may be hard to take it off when organizational realignment or peace is declared.

Let's Interface!   Another way to knock down walls is to walk through them. By this I mean to physically go across the borders, to visit the other departments, to show your face to the people you interface with. Most of us know each other as voices on the phone, names on memos, or code numbers on faxes. One rule of thumb here isn't new, but is more important today: It's hard to attack someone you know personally. As long as you're a voice or a name or a number, you can be treated miserably, but when you're a real live human, this is less apt to happen. Get out of your office, go meet and visit. Become a face, not a fax.

Unlearn ————————————————————————————————

Continued survival demands new skills, approaches, definitions, and processes. You simply can't count on the ideas or methods that seemed to work in the past, or that are working today. All of us should be willing to *unlearn* yesterday's wisdom when it's inappropriate. The theme of the adaptive is, That was then, this is now. One tip: Stay clear of the whiner's anthem—"But we always did it this way," or "Under the old system..." or "We used to...." Instead, start using the new terminology, the new names, and the new phrases. Identify yourself with the winners, not the holdouts. Otherwise, you might be asked to man the light switch!

At a recent meeting of the Supreme Soviet, one of the governing bodies in the U.S.S.R. undergoing *perestroika*, a supporter of Gorbachev's reforms referred to his opponent, a hard-liner, as a "Stalin-brain." "We have two types of people here," he said, "forward thinkers and Stalin-brains." Stalin-brains can't unlearn. I'm sure you're not one of them. They don't read books like this.

Turn Enemies Into Friends _____

Suppliers are joining buyers, manufacturers are joining customers, competitors are buying each other, and all sorts of
strategic alliances are being formed in response to today's
new economic climates. In addition to permanent combinations (mergers, acquisitions), people and groups from separate organizations are combining temporarily for a particular
project or product. Even when the companies involved main-
tain their own identities and futures, blended work groups
are springing up among them—cooperating so they can
jointly compete against the real enemies: mediocrity, failure,
and waste.

Getting the Real Enemy.   For all the competition we've been
hearing about, cooperation is on the rise. Companies aren't
the only ones cooperating. People are cooperating across
once-isolated, functional departments. They're actually
learning that in order to *compete externally*, companies are
having to *cooperate internally*. They're learning that the enemy isn't the engineering department but the Japanese (or
Germans, or Taiwanese, or Swedes, or Americans).

Knowing how to adapt to these combinations and work
within them is a critical success factor in your career. Make
every effort to understand and share the concerns of other
groups. Learn their language, their jargon, their priorities
and proclivities. Show interest in what they do. Don't judge
or analyze while you're learning, either. And don't forget to
Listen. This even helps deal with the Stalin-brains among
them: In their view, you become more "us" and less "them."
You also reduce your chances of getting shot.

Fight Smart!   Because you'll be working across organizational boundaries more and more and in unfamiliar or even
unprotected circumstances, I've three more suggestions
here:

1. Don't fight someone else's battle (like your boss's).

2. Don't fight for others unless they're fighting just as hard (remember Stan?).

3. Don't inherit internal feuds.

When a problem erupts, avoid making it an "us vs. them" problem. Turn the problem into a third party, asking how both of you can work together to defeat the problem, not each other. And always remember that the vendor you stiff-armed, the department head you shunned, or the competitor you offended might end up being your boss, your customer, or your partner. Change makes strange bedfellows.

Erase Borders, Grow People

This technique applies to your relationships with people who work for you: your staff, assistants, or crew. The message for everyone in a supervisory or management position today is, Let people develop. They are today's most adaptive resource. Don't confine them, and don't underestimate them. So far we've covered personal advice, ways *you* can adapt. But keep in mind that no one succeeds or fails individually anymore. More than most of us would like, we're very dependent on the performance of others. And our relationship with each of them is also subject to change. The idea that people once working for you will always work for you is no longer valid.

These are two reasons to give those working for you plenty of room to grow. If you're going anywhere in today's business world, you're going as a group. Each of us needs all the help he or she can get. Empowering others, allowing them to grow and develop, is not an interesting management alternative. It's the way you win. Controlling them, exploiting them, and commanding them are out. Those are the methods of the Stalin-brains.

Raise the Bar

Expect continual improvement in your quest for excellence. As soon as a goal is met, "raise the bar," just like a high jumper who masters a certain height. Keep setting ever-higher goals. Complacency is the enemy of the adaptive. Excellence is not a final destination; it's a process of continual improvement. Keep going, keep growing, and keep getting better. That's what adapting is all about.

When I walk into a company, it usually takes me less than an hour to pick out the comers, the ones on the way up. They follow some old but very appropriate advice: They look, dress, talk, and think about two jobs above them. If they're department managers, you couldn't tell them from division managers, or vice presidents. They adopt the styles and methods appropriate for higher positions before they get to them. They're paving the way for advancement. They want the distinction between where they are and where they want to be to disappear. They don't get up in the morning and say, "Well, I'm a department manager, so I should look and dress like one." They say, "I'm going to look, dress, and act for the job I want, not the one I have."

Going Out to Go Up.   On a personal note, the best way to raise the bar is often to move outside the company—to sample the job market and find out how other employers view you. Always know where you stand in terms of value, compensation, and attractiveness to others. Stay alert to outside opportunities. Don't fool yourself. The odds are that within a few years at most, you'll be seriously looking for a move. I've heard dozens of people tell me they couldn't make more outside, wouldn't be able to find a job, or couldn't afford to make the move. All they're doing is *lowering* the bar, not raising it. Keep tabs—constantly—on what you could make, who's hiring, and what they're looking for. Sometimes you outgrow your company and need to move to the bigger leagues. When I say raise the bar, I'm suggesting that you might get to the point where the next higher bar is in another stadium. Go for it.

Use Shock Therapy on Your Boss.   Another tip: Look for ways to surprise those above you and shatter their stereotypes of you. Let's face it—all of us have a reputation or are otherwise pegged by those above us. We're expected to think and act a certain way because we're only at a certain level. I suggest you carefully study higher concerns and address them to your management. If you're at a meeting and are expected to represent a department's position, take the role of division advocate: "I'd like to address ways this prospect will affect the division." Do your homework, and the result will be a new you. Appearances are vital in the quest for advancement and growth. If you start concerning yourself in a very visible way with higher issues, you make yourself eligible for higher positions.

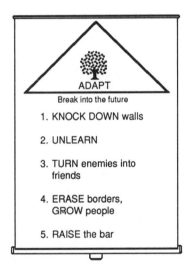

ADAPT

Break into the future

1. KNOCK DOWN walls

2. UNLEARN

3. TURN enemies into friends

4. ERASE borders, GROW people

5. RAISE the bar

Barriers to Breaking Into the Future

The definition of *adapt* holds both a promise and a price. The promise is a better fit to new demands, but the price is high: "often by modification." Here is the problem: Individuals and organizations must change to adapt, and change is upsetting, frightening, and arduous for both individuals and groups. It's almost always met with resistance.

The human race is one of the most adaptive species on the face of the earth. We live in the tropics and the arctic circles, in valleys and on mountains, in deserts and among rain forests. Why can't we be so versatile and adaptive in our organizations? Is it because the law of natural selection affects our species (adapt or die out) but not our companies or institutions? Think again. We can't adapt when we can't change, when the barriers are too high. Not adapting condemns us to the past, or to the present—which is fast becoming the past. The law does apply to us: *Adapt or die*. What keeps losers from following this mandate? Here are my choices for the five highest barriers.

1. Fear of Loss.   If you cling to the *features* of an organizational position or job, you'll see change as a risk, a chance to lose something. You won't want to trade what you know you have for what you might get in the bargain. Adapters turn this around. They emphasize what's to be gained by adapting—and what's to be lost by not adapting.

One technique from the Prospect Pathway can be used here. Remember "Pretend it's fixed"? When confronting change, I suggest you "pretend it's done." Pretend the change has come to pass and look back on what you might have lost in the process. Chances are you won't miss it. You'll realize you never had it in the first place, or you'll realize how insignificant it really was. The old saying, "You never know what you have until it's gone," also needs revision. In many cases, "You never know how little you've lost until it's gone."

2. Lack of Effort.   Change is messy, uncertain, and difficult. It seems much easier to stay the same. But this is how death occurs—a giving up. Don't think the easiest way to meet change is to ignore it. It's often more difficult to resist than to accept, and holding on to what's known can be a fool's game, not to mention a terrible burden.

3. Future Ghosts.   Future ghosts are what people imagine can go wrong. Some people like to predict failure before any change—to think of all that can go wrong—and therefore choose to stay the same—the "safe" alternative. They don't "pretend it's fixed or changed"; they "pretend it fails." They never seem to realize what can go wrong with staying the same. They criticize what might be, but not what is.

When you're innovating, the "what-if" exercise helps. You ask yourself or others, "What if we tried it backwards?" or "What if we turned it inside out?" and so on. But change-resisters (the Stalin-brains, the desk huggers, the whiners) play the what-if game differently. They ask, "What if it *doesn't* work?" and "What if it's *not* perfect." They don't whine over what is lost. They whine over what might be lost. Seems kind of dumb, doesn't it?

If you find yourself falling into this trap, remember that *everything* can go wrong, especially continuing to do what you think is going right. Future ghosts are easy to imagine, but 90 percent will never materialize. And finally, suppose your bleak forecasts are correct? Suppose the change won't work. So what? Are you better off because you called it? Or are you seen as a whiner, a martyr, or the "I-told-you-so." Sometimes people can't be dissuaded from a new venture by logic alone. They've got to experience what will go wrong before they learn. Let them. Your job is to survive change, not to prevent others from getting burned by it. *Save yourself.* If they won't listen to you, don't push it. Let them listen to pain.

4. Underestimation. Here's how we lose before we start, because we underestimate our personal or joint powers to adapt. We underestimate our people, our flexibility, our strengths. And we overestimate the difficulties. But most commonly, we underestimate the power of the forces of change—what we're up against. Always remember that reasons to change need not be logical, prudent, or even attractive. Change has its own momentum, rational or not. Don't get run over by it.

5. Waiting Until it Goes Away. The ostrich follows this advice, and so does an army in a defensive posture. The purpose of a defensive perimeter in warfare is to protect those hiding within it from a temporary threat. But the need to adapt is not always a threat, nor is it temporary. Even the ostrich must come up for air sooner or later. Even the entrenched troops must come out for a look. The world will not go away. We will, if we don't adapt to it.

Here are other reasons to join the parade of change rather than stand by and wait until it passes. Even if the change eventually fizzles out, you've hurt yourself by leaving long-lasting impressions on others. You're remembered as a whiner, a wet blanket, or just someone who doesn't count. Even if the change is no more than a fleeting fad, destined to fade, you can use it as a stepping-stone to better assignments, acquaintances, and exposure. And failed changes have benefits too. They build relationships among those who shared the experience (the bonding of survivors), they make careers, and they open new opportunities. In other words, joining change might not pay off because the train never arrives at its intended destination, but you can jump off along the way—and end up in a better place.

1. Fear of LOSS

2. Lack of EFFORT

3. FUTURE GHOSTS

4. UNDERESTIMATION

5. WAITING until it goes away

The Process Is the Goal

This is perhaps the most important lesson behind the need to adapt. *Adapting is a process.* The very *process* of trying new methods, learning and unlearning, making new connections, new relationships, and building new skills *is the goal*. The process of adapting should be unending. You should always be increasing your agility, your versatility, and your options. If you visualize your career as a journey, as a continuous process of growth and improvement, you'll be looking for every opportunity to adapt, to change, to make yourself fit for new applications. Remember, no one else is doing this for you anymore, if they ever did.

Each of us is on a journey, and even though the destination might be obscure or unpredictable, the process can be structured and meaningful if you choose to make it so. And the process can be learned. You can be more comfortable along the way, more secure, and more successful if you unlearn what's holding you back and learn these ways to adjust when conditions require—to shift, to pivot, to adapt—to keep going *fast-forward*.

What to Do Once You Stand Out From the Rest

If you take these first five Pathways seriously and look for ways to put them to use on your journey, you'll end up moving ahead when so many others around you are lost, tired, or blocked. You also begin to realize that you're in a minority: most people don't know the Pathways. Regardless of where you work or what you do for a living, you'll see opportunities for leadership everywhere, and you'll find yourself poised to take them. You'll find yourself on the next Pathway, the final one: Lead.

PictoGame—Round 5

The symbol of the Adapt Pathway is a growing tree. I find the biological metaphor of growth very appropriate when describing adaptation in business settings. When a tree or any other living thing stops growing, it stops living. The same applies to each of us, although we encounter restrictions and barriers all around us. Some common ones are shown in the pictograms on the next page. See if you can identify each barrier to growth shown there, then check my suggestions on pages 174–175.

WHAT'S WRONG WITH THESE PICTURES?

1. _____

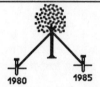

2. _____

3. _____

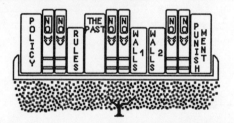

4. _____

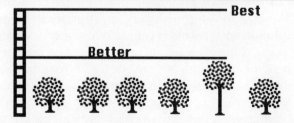

5. _____

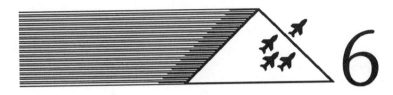

6

Break Out in Front

Leaders win, watchers lose.

The *Lead* Pathway

Having the Right Stuff at the Right Time

You are standing in the middle of a leadership vacuum. No matter where you work or what you do there, the forces of change are creating tremendous new opportunities for you, pulling you toward leadership. The business world is begging for leaders, everywhere, at all levels, and if you can put the lessons of the previous Pathways to use, you will be one. It's a seller's market for those who have the goods—the material of leadership. Buyers are everywhere, the supply is short, and the rewards are high. And you are uniquely positioned to receive them.

Leading is the natural destination in our sequence of six Pathways. Here is where you'll combine what you've learned and take a quantum leap to higher levels of survival, satisfaction, and success. The lessons of leadership have been woven into each of the previous chapters, built into each of the Pathways. You're almost at the payoff. You're at leadership's door. It's time to recognize how close you are, to feel the power of leading that is inside you, and to exercise it. It's time to learn to Lead.

Leading Is Leverage

Leading is nothing more than effecting outcomes through others. So far our Pathways have been targeted on you and your skills: how to listen, how to innovate, and so forth. Now you need to leverage those skills and perceptions through other people, to multiply your effect, your influence, your power. The concept of *leverage* fits leadership very well. When you use a lever and a fulcrum to move a heavy object, you're doing something way beyond your unaided power. You could never move a two-ton rock with your bare hands, but put a pole, a stick, or a board under it and pry it up and you've used leverage. Leverage is also used as a financial multiplier. When you make a 20 percent down payment on a house, you're getting the entire house for only one-fifth of the price. You're using a small amount of your own funds to make the deal move. If the house appreciates in value over time, you get 100 percent of the appreciation with only 20 percent of the investment. That's leverage: using a little to get a lot. And if you had the entire purchase price, you could put 20 percent down on five houses rather than all of it on one, getting five times the appreciation. If you think of leverage as a way of multiplying your effect, of leveraging what you know and can do through others, you've got a good idea of what leadership is all about.

Harnessing the Potential Energy
All Around You

There is another significant parallel here. In both cases, moving the rock and multiplying your purchasing power, you don't have to do anything unusual, illegal, or heroic. You just put the existing ingredients of leverage to work for you. The tools of leverage are available and the principles are well known. All you have to do is apply them. That's what this chapter is all about: applying known techniques to existing conditions. The potential for change is all around you. The rules of change are known. Put them together and you're a leader.

Leading is different, then, from commanding or controlling others. Leaders don't force events or people. They *allow* events and *empower* people. They cause change and improvement by releasing forces that already exist in circumstances that have already been created.

Leading Is Releasing
What Already Exists

Forces of change are pressing on all sides of modern corporations, which themselves are straining at every seam. The structures of the past are proving unable to withstand the pressure, and new ones are evolving with terrific speed. The methods of the past are proving unacceptable, the techniques that once worked are failing, and the people within these organizations aren't satisfied as easily as their predecessors. Even in organizations seeming to resist change, the forces are being stored like energy in a spring, ready to be released at the right moment by the right person. In one way or another, each organization, large or small, is cocked and ready for the right finger on the delicate trigger mechanism.

Customers who want better service are yearning for the company that can provide it. Departments that have outgrown their missions are longing for a redefinition of what they should be doing. Competitors are taunting your company to meet them or match them, if you dare. Individuals are straining to do more, to contribute more, and to realize their ever-expanding potential within the confines of organizational structures and job descriptions grown too restrictive. Better processes and more innovative ideas are inches away from materializing but for the right conditions. The potential energy of change comes in all sorts of sizes and types, and it is everywhere waiting for leaders to release it, to guide it, to leverage it to great accomplishments.

Leaders don't invent the future. They allow us to enter it under our own power. They step into a setting full of unrealized expectations and untapped power and light the fuse. The energy is released, the potential becomes kinetic, and the change is done. That's the magic of leadership. You don't have to create the conditions for change, or design the mechanisms that carry it out. In most cases, leaders simply find the dynamite and light the fuse.

Lighting the Fuse, Leading the Parade

When Ronald Reagan was swept to his presidential landslide, he hadn't created a resurgence of conservatism in the United States, he hadn't engineered a rebirth of national pride, coordinated a demand for tax reform, given birth to a new work ethic, or stimulated individual or group greed. All these conditions were in place. As one political observer noted, he simply found the parade and stepped in front of it. Or according to another, he rode the horse in the direction it was going.

Leaders tap into what already exists. They harness powers already beginning to show. They look for evidence of these powers, stimulate them, and release them. The most photogenic, idealistic, charismatic candidates for leadership wouldn't make it championing communism as the economic future of eastern Europe—wrong time, wrong movement, no energy, no parade. Electricians, playwrights, music professors, and artists are being sucked into leadership vacuums there. They know which way the horses are running.

Your company is full of horses straining at the bit, wondering which direction to run, and waiting for permission to bolt. If you lack leaders, the anguish can be palpable. Pent up forces without release have been known to lead to breakdowns, illness, even explosions. But once harnessed, leveraged, and let go, they can lead to tremendous improvement, advancement, and competitive advantage. By lighting the fuse, by releasing the energy, by allowing what *can be to be*, ordinary people become leaders.

We're Not Talking Magic Here

That's the main message, the one I'd like you to remember above all others here. Leading isn't difficult, it isn't magic, and it isn't reserved for the elite. Leading doesn't require years of training, mountains of hard work, or the luck of being in the right place at the right time. It requires perceptive people who recognize forces of change, straining discontent, and capabilities extending beyond the current boundaries of structure and conduct. Leaders find these and release them. They unleash them, let them go, and point them in the right direction. Sometimes the result is startling, dramatic, and surprising. Sometimes it's gradual, an easing of tension, an accommodation more than a revolution. In any case, nothing of significance happens without a leader, any leader. I take that back. One thing happens without a leader: *management*. But management is not even a close cousin to leadership.

Managing Isn't Leading

Since organizations do exist to let many people achieve few goals, some governing mechanism is always necessary. All societies, groups, companies, and cultures have rules, restrictions, and preferred modes of behavior. What they are and how they're applied vary tremendously, however. Two extremes exist in today's corporations, governments, and institutions: *management* and *leadership*. If you know the difference, if you understand when one is called for and not the other, a lot of the confusion over how organizations should run disappears. Let's contrast these two diverging positions so that the differences can stand out in sharp relief.

Why Management Is Not Leadership

- Management is the process of controlling and optimizing what exists.

- Management is for stability.

- Management is transactional.

- Managers follow rules, assure compliance with them, and correct conditions that deviate from standards.

- Managers contain.

- Managers handle the *how* of work.

- Leadership is the process of changing what exists to what is needed.

- Leadership is for change.

- Leadership is transformational.

- Leaders break rules, make new ones, encourage creativity, and destroy restraints and inhibitions that keep behavior within outmoded standards.

- Leaders release.

- Leaders handle the *what*, the *why*, and the *who*.

It's easy to see why, in times of turmoil, we need fewer managers and more leaders. The vacuum is growing.

Suppose your organization is a railroad line. The engineer running the train is in a management position. He or she keeps the trains well-fueled, lubricated, repaired, maintained, and running on time. If something out of the ordinary arises, managers jump on it and stamp it out—it's a deviation, an interference, a break in the program. Managers keep the system running, with constant monitoring, supervision, and checking. They reward others who contribute to the smooth operation of the line and the trains and punish or remove those who interfere. They preserve, protect, and extend what already exists: the tracks, engines, cars.

What happens when the line starts losing passengers? When airline travel takes a bite out of the market? When the towns the line serves start to die? Or when a competitor builds a parallel line and uses more luxurious cars with better service? Forces of change impact the railroad, and a call for leadership louder than the locomotive's whistle should be sounded. Now the game has changed. We no longer win by keeping things going smoothly, by following the rules, by protecting what is. What is doesn't cut it. Who can tell us what's needed? Who can help us get it? Leaders, not managers. The managers can come back when the new equilibrium point is obtained, when the new routes have been mapped out, the trees have been cut, the new track laid, and the new cars delivered. Then it's time to settle down and manage—when the rules are written, when the route is known, when the risks are predictable, and when the stakes are incremental. Not when they're quantum. Not during times of transition, transformation, or turmoil. Those are times that demand leaders. Those are the terms that describe our time.

The Leadership Vacuum _____

Stable times stifle leaders. They hate conformity and rigidity, and they're too impatient to wait for a death or a retirement to leave room for growth. They yearn to make opportunities, not to wait for them. They like difference and diversity, uncovering what's hidden. These are all very human traits, ones that have led us to invent, innovate, risk, travel, explore, and grow. We're born with them. But the sad part is that these human sparks never become flames in stable times. They sputter for lack of tinder. They're stamped out by the guarantors of the status quo.

Give a company a few years of stability and success and you'll see this phenomenon at work. Upsetting ideas are quashed, aspirations are dampened, dreams are dulled. People who want change are stymied, stultified. Rules and procedures dominate, and survivors are those who comply with them, who learn them, follow them to the letter, and make sure others do the same. These people rise to the top. They make it there by obeying, protecting, and preserving. We call them managers. The last thing they want is change. The last thing they'll tolerate is leadership. They might call themselves leaders, but they're really no different from prison guards. They're paid to keep a lid on things, to keep them exactly as they are. Sooner or later, however, the forces of change become too great, too powerful to be contained. The lid blows off. Turmoil ensues.

America: Land Where the Lids Are Blowing Off

That scenario isn't fictional. It's a concise history of American enterprise from the end of World War II to the present. The lids are blowing off everywhere now, and the management mindset is puzzled and scared. Some fight back, hoping to hold the waves of change at bay like the Dutch boy with a finger in the dike. They intensify their command and control mechanisms, bracing against change by applying the same old rules in the same old way—the way of stability. They supervise more closely, punish more severely, and order more loudly. They're losing. It is a new game now, and the rules have changed. You don't win by managing, you win by leading. You don't win by capping the pressure, you win by releasing it, guiding it, directing it, harnessing it.

If you're a fan of stability, consistency, and control, you should start working on a time machine, one that will take you back to the 1950s. If you're a fan of change, you were born in the right era.

Living in the Age of Leadership _____

These are indeed exciting times for leaders at all levels. New organizations are springing up; new relationships among companies are being formed, a new labor force, diverse and fresh, is entering the market. Companies are forming new visions, building new strategies, and confronting the unknown, using the untested to meet the uncertain every day. It is the age of leadership. We need leaders at all levels—in the boardroom, on the shop floor, in the factories, in the back offices, and on the front lines facing competitors and customers every day—leaders who can help the rest of us make it through change, help us find the pathways, and guide us along them. How does one become such a person? How do you learn to be a leader? What's the cost?

The wonderful part about leading is that it's a completely open field. There aren't any entrance exams, educational requirements, licenses, or restrictions. Anybody can be one. Leadership is self-affirming: You do it so you are it. And it's not a rare opportunity, either. We tend to think of leaders as a lonely few at the top. Not so anymore. Whenever more than one person gathers in the name of change, a leader is born. They define themselves by their action, not by their title or job description. They might lead for a while, then back off and manage. They might follow others through some changes, then jump to the front. Leading isn't a job title. It's a way of thinking and acting. And it can be learned.

The Collapse of Control _____

The trends aren't coaxing leaders out of the closet. They're blasting them out. The call is too compelling to ignore. The downward flow of responsibility is helping. So is the collapse of control mechanisms. Controls keep activities running smoothly. They surface variances from plans or standards and help management correct them. Controls are the apparatus of stability. We know them as policies, procedures, job descriptions, instructions, standards, performance reports, evaluations, appraisals, and the like. When things are predictable, controls can be designed and enforced with little trouble. When times are changing, controls fall apart. As soon as they are designed and applied, the work changes, the goals are revised, the work force is different, or the tools we use to work are modified. Controls have a hell of a time keeping up with change. They might still be there, but their meaningfulness isn't.

Leading Spring-Loaded, Day-Glo Workers

When the people who make up the organization remain the same, and when they're homogeneous, alike, and consistent, they're easy to manage. They think the same, have the same values, and generally behave the same. The word *herd* comes to mind. But when they're made up of varying types of people, of all ages, backgrounds, cultures, and beliefs, they're tougher to manage. They don't all have the same buttons to push. They don't respond to the same rewards. They don't fear the same punishments. What makes a 50-year-old white male jump might not even cause a blink with a 20-year-old Hispanic female. The same whip won't make everybody flinch. The same carrot won't make everyone salivate. Controls collapse.

Diversity also brings the fuel of change with it. New ideas, different perspectives, fresh viewpoints, unusual strengths, and heretofore untapped skills exist. When the organization was a thousand middle-class men in gray flannel suits, the ideas were made of gray flannel. Now they come in silk, linen, spandex, denim, corduroy, and burlap. And they're red, blue, fuchsia; they're paisley, striped, and day-glo. And they're in motion, a continuous swirl of new people, new ideas, unusual approaches. All are set in motion and powered by the desire to make a difference, to have an impact on their surroundings, and to build an individual identity. It's

not a melting pot, it's a boiling pot, fired by rising expectations, anxiety, impatience with the present, and concern for
the future. Spring-loaded for change. Waiting for the leaders
to emerge and pull the trigger. A powerful, idea-rich, talent-
laden parade—waiting for someone to get in front of it and
lead it.

What People Expect From Leaders

Because most companies are living with one foot in the past
and one in the present, the role of "leader" is seldom created
through normal channels. Nobody comes to your desk and
asks you if you've applied for the new leader position. Leadership roles aren't made for you, you make them yourself.
You don't wait for them, you take them. And you don't have
to accept the ones thrust in front of you. Some are couched
in leadership terms, but they're really kamikaze deals, or va-
cancies for the role of guinea pig or scapegoat. You can get
sucked into a leadership role, and you can also get sucked
into a black hole, never to be seen again. I want you to know
when and how to lead. I want you to realize that there's a lot
of nonsense surrounding the term, a lot of myths and misconceptions. Most of all, you need to know what the job requires, what you're in for. Here I'll explain what most people
expect of a good leader. Then I'll review what they don't
want from you.

First, the expectations.

Vision. I'll start with this term not because it's popular or
trendy, but because it's so wrongly interpreted. The working
definition is something like *being able to see into the future*,
over the horizon, or beyond the sight of everyone else. Nothing could be more misleading. Every January the supermar-
ket tabloids are packed with foolish utterances of people who
claim to predict the future, to have vision. We certainly don't
call these people visionaries. We call them kooks. Leaders
aren't visionaries. They don't predict the future. They make

the future. And they make it by visualizing what it can be, not what it will be.

The metaphor of sight tricks us here. Vision only works in a straight line. Even the most farsighted can only claim to see in a direct path. But leaders are different. They have the knack of seeing around corners, of seeing what *can* happen.

An old science-fiction story described a character who could see fifteen minutes into the future. It doesn't seem like much, but imagine how quickly you could make it to the closest race track if you were so gifted! Leaders who Listen and Prospect see the future while it's still under development. They see it in sharp relief, standing out from the background while others are standing still and looking down at their shoes.

The visualization of what change can do separates leaders from most everyone else. They play a game similar to one of the Prospecting tricks. They play "Let's pretend it works." Then they start imagining how the future will be if it works, even if it's just fifteen minutes ahead. Leaders don't see into the future. They live in the future. Skeptics play a different variation of the game. They play "Let's pretend it doesn't work." And they can get pretty creative when finding fault with a proposed or imminent change. Not too many people follow skeptics. Skeptics practice failure. Leaders rehearse success.

Elgan Baker is a friend of mine from back in high school. When I met him at a reunion, he described his work as director of the Indiana Center for psychoanalysis. An associate professor in the department of psychiatry at Indiana University School of Medicine, Elgan has a thriving practice in "creative visualization." He works with many teams in the NBA and NFL by helping star athletes visualize a completed pass, a three-point shot, or a slam-dunk over the fiercest defender. It works, they claim, because you can't be good at something you can't imagine. In fact, research is showing that not only do the athletes experience cognitive (knowing) preparation, their motor neurons actually fire during this visualization process. That means they're not only preparing for success, they're *physically practicing, learning* success. That's another secret of leadership. Leaders don't just prepare for success by seeing into the future, they practice success while they're looking.

So seeing or visualizing success is the first step, the critical step, towards achieving it. When you do it, it shows, and others around you pay attention and follow. Seeing around corners, thinking in terms of accomplished change, and visualizing the roles, activities, and relationships in the changed conditions are the exercises of leaders. If you want to lead, you've got to go in advance. Visualization lets you do this. It's just a short step from visualizing the future, even if it's just around the corner, to creating the future.

Risking.   Risking means taking chances and being prepared to lose. Can you imagine a leader who risks nothing, who wants you or your friends to run over the hill into the enemy's fire while he huddles in the bunker? All over the world, managers are huddling, asking subordinates to accept change while showing no willingness to risk themselves, their authority, their comfort, perks, position, or security. This is the legacy of a generation of executives bred on stability. And it's another characteristic of the transformation of business: those who think in terms of the old trying to cope with the new, and often using the troops as cannon fodder.

Today's workers are naturally jaded. They've seen relatives, friends, and coworkers come back from change on stretchers. And they're not too excited about risk unless the ones in charge put something of their own on the line. You can't expect others to embrace change without embracing it yourself—first.

Being a leader doesn't mean you have to expose your chest to the first bullets of change. In fact, being a laggard achieves this. It's the ones who don't move, who don't get with the new who are in danger. Smart leaders don't play "What if it doesn't work?" They play "What if we don't try it?" They enunciate the dangers of staying the same, hiding from

change, or resisting it. They point out what's at risk with the
past and the present, not with the future.

Take your situation. Why don't you sit down right now and
make a list of the things you'd like to change about your company. Are you perfectly content with everything you do, how
you do it, and how well you're rewarded? Is absolutely everything about your job, your company, and its management out-
standing, above reproach, beyond improvement? I doubt it. To
one extent or another, some things are done wrong, some work
is stupid, some people are incompetent, some conditions are
unsatisfactory, and some procedures are wasteful—everywhere.
That's present risk—the danger of staying the same. Without
change, everyone is engaged in risking every day. There is no
escaping risk, even when you do nothing. Leaders don't recklessly bet on the future. They just don't recklessly bet on the
present. They bet on what they can create or influence—what's
around the corner. No one can create or influence the past. We
inherited what we have. We can *make* what we need, but only if
we're willing to risk.

Information-Sharing. Fear of the future, of change, is
grounded in uncertainty, a lack of information about the future. Changing means trading what's known for what isn't,
and unless what's known (the present situation) is pure hell,
the future can seem a bum deal. Leaders know that people
will accept a deal if the payoff is greater than the pain, if the
gain is more than the loss. But if the gain is unknown or
questionable and the pain, the cost of changing, is well
known, it's tough to convince people to trade one for the
other. Start by making the changed environment known. Remove the mystery, the smoke and mirrors. Bring the future
into the present by describing it and letting people test it, feel
it, and know it. This is the role of information: making what's
unknown known.

No one knows everything about a proposed change—a reorganization, merger, downsizing, or automation project, to
name a few. But we can determine its *boundaries*. We can de-

scribe what the change will be like, even if this means telling when it will occur, who will be affected, why it's needed, how it will be managed, and what to expect as it progresses. And most importantly, we can tell what *won't* change—what's safe, secure, outside the scope, or beyond the reach of current plans. Describing what won't change is just as important as describing what will. It eliminates unfounded rumors, suspicion, and fear. The more information a leader can give, the more he or she can help others visualize and live in the future. That's leverage. That's leading.

Involvement. Today's workers don't like to have things done to them. They won't buy into an idea unless they have some say in it, some involvement in designing it. Leaders make the idea, the change, the future reach out and touch everyone. They answer the first question on everyone's mind: What's in this for me? Don't let anyone spectate, sit in the bleachers and watch. Get them involved. Make the future, the change, theirs. Make their roles meaningful and mandatory. Anyone can criticize a team while sitting in the stands. Few can do so when on the field, wearing the team's uniform.

Some of the biggest failures I've seen prove this axiom. When top executives come up with a new direction, plan it out, even give it a fancy name, then force it on the organization as a fait accompli, a take-it-or-leave-it deal, they lose. They ask for resistance because they don't provide for assistance. It's either one or the other: People who aren't involved fight change; and those who are involved help make it happen. In the game of Turmoil, no one should be allowed to watch. Watching, not participating, is the same as resisting. As Mr. Joe so correctly said, "No one should leave the ring without a bloody face" (well, at least a sweaty face).

Energy. Leaders don't have to be tall, handsome, beautiful, young, slim, or strong. They don't need the looks of Gregory Peck, the voice of Ronald Reagan, or the forcefulness of Lee

Iacocca. What about Mother Teresa? How slim and handsome is Lech Walesa? Even Mikhail Gorbachev is little more than a modern caricature of Nikita Kruschev: short, bald, and blemished. Appearances aren't important. What you look like and sound like are inconsequential. It's what you move like that counts—your energy and excitement.

In his classic discourse known to us as *The Republic,* Plato envisioned a nation of philosopher-kings who contemplated the proper meaning of events and engaged in long discussions of proper actions to take in light of them. Since his fantasies, I know of not one philosopher who became a great leader. Sure, there are leaders who contemplate and philosophize. But no one can get behind an idle contemplator, a speculator. No one follows a slow, lethargic, or inactive leader—no matter how smart or wise he or she may be. Motion is what's called for here, particularly when the stakes are being doubled and the space invaders are set on crunching us to death. Leaders show high energy that stimulates contagious excitement. How else would we follow them? How inspiring is someone who's bored, lazy, or content? Cows should be content. Leaders should be constantly in motion—making the future happen.

High Expectations. Can you imagine a leader who calls out to the group, "OK, everybody, let's get out there and be mediocre"? Not too inspiring, is it? Sometimes high expectations aren't reached, but on the other hand, low expectations are almost always reached. Asking others to achieve little almost guarantees that little will be achieved. Low expectations are self-fulfilling.

If you've read many biographies of successful individuals, one element of their backgrounds stands out in sharp relief. Sometime in their lives someone told them they could achieve more, that they were destined to go places and do great things. A teacher, parent, counselor, or employer gave them high expectations. Of course the converse is also common. Not too many people do well if they're told they can't, won't, or shouldn't. People who are told they're worthless generally turn out that way. This is not always the case, but certainly enough times to prove the adage, You can't be what you think yourself incapable of being. Leaders make us aim high.

Leading means setting high expectations and expecting others to meet them. The new buzzwords are "stretch objectives" but the idea behind them isn't new. Here again the role of leading is little more than releasing, letting others strive toward goals themselves. Often the only factor missing is the goal. If you provide it, and if you make it real, you're leading.

Recognition.   Leaders are entrusted with the hopes of others. These hopes are projected from individuals to the leader when the individuals trust the leader to care for them. The leader, in turn, must project recognition and concern back to the individuals. This is the two-way street of leadership. If you don't recognize the existence or the aspirations of others, they're not likely to recognize your role as leader. Recognize their strengths, concerns, fears, and hopes. Show them you recognize them. No one can ignore others and be followed by them at the same time. Leaders are the guardians, the trustees of others' futures. To lead them, you must recognize them, and their capacity to hope. If listening is the first step toward responding (Chapter 4), recognizing the message and the sender is the first step toward leading.

Motion.   Leaders create difference. They set the new into motion. Planning, preparing, and rehearsing are important prerequisites to effective action, in times of change or not. But action is what announces change, what pulls it from the future to the present, what converts it from a vague abstraction to a concrete reality. Leaders are always in motion, making waves, kicking up dust. When the pain of changing is felt, when the struggle begins to tire, when the goals begin to fade, the leader keeps spinning, like the flywheel of change.

Organizational inertia is the greatest enemy of a learning,

improving group. Effective leaders never flag, never sit, and never stop fighting this inertia. A leader's motion is the signal that inertia hasn't won. When people pushing a heavy object begin to tire, their eyes are cast downward. When people pushing a change begin to tire, their eyes are raised to the leader, looking for signals. Is it over? Have we lost? If the leader is still, the answer is yes.

How Good People Become Bad Leaders

What works against leadership? What keeps well-intentioned, hard-working, and genuine people from becoming effective leaders? I'll point out the five most common barriers to leading later, but here I'd like to discuss otherwise meritable characteristics, good qualities, that may make you a very likable, respected person but a terrible leader. Here's how good people become bad leaders. Here's what people expect from everyone *but* their leaders.

Love. We want our leaders to recognize us, respect us, involve us, and represent us, but we don't want them to love us. Love connotes an unconditional acceptance of another as he or she exists. Our leaders can't get us to change if they love us as we are. Leaders release the energy to improve by making us unsatisfied with the way we are, the way we work, the results we achieve. Leaders instill dissatisfaction with the present. It's not a hateful dissatisfaction, more an expectant one. They expect us to be better and encourage us to be different. Can you imagine telling your loved one, "I'm dissatisfied with the way you are. I expect you to be better, and I want you to change?"

We don't want leaders to fawn over us, slobber over us, or hug us. We want them to let us reach our fullest potential, to show us the way around obstacles, to pull us through the rough spots, and to look around corners for change. We can get love from our spouses or intimate friends. Leaders give us the future.

Supervision. Warren Bennis, coauthor of *Leaders, The*

Strategies for Taking Charge, said it so well: "Managers do things right. Leaders *do the right things*." Managers are there to help others focus on what they're doing, while leaders are there to help us focus on what we're not doing—on what we could be doing instead. They shouldn't watch us, monitor us, check on us, or correct us. They should compel us, pull us into the future—the place where they live. We don't need them peering over our shoulder. We need them peering over our future.

Naiveté.   Expect leaders to be honest, frank, and realistic. Cheerleaders and dreamers shouldn't apply. The future is going to be tough, the price of survival and success is going to be high, and some simply won't make it through the transition. Those who do will find themselves paying for the passage in more ways than one. Anybody who doesn't freely admit this is living in Fantasyland. I'll follow a leader into the future if he or she has the sense to know stupidity, greed, selfishness, and just plain bull when they see it. I won't follow a grinning idiot who keeps alive the saying that "ignorance is bliss." I want my leaders to have their eyes wide open and their critical abilities well focused.

When the opportunity to lead comes, keep this in mind. Start by admitting the difficulties and accepting the challenge. If it's going to be tough as hell, say so. If it means some comforting ways are getting tossed out, admit this. Today's workers don't expect miracles or free rides. They're willing to pay if you're wise enough to name the price. Only drunks and the demented are undaunted. They're quite willing to stumble ahead. Fortunately, no one follows.

Servitude.   Change that isn't earned doesn't take. It slides off like an oyster on Teflon. Leaders don't give change to others the way a servant would give his master his coat. Despite the obvious reasons dealing with position and lack of respect, serving up the new on a silver platter virtually assures it will be rejected or ignored. Leading means letting others realize their full potential, not giving it to them gift wrapped.

Anyone who's seen the difference between a teenage boy who saves and slaves for his first car and one who has it presented to him knows this. Working for it makes all the difference in the world.

Today's employees are much more self-sufficient and self-directed. They aren't children. They don't need their food cut up for them, nor do they want a doting leader telling them what's best for them. They want the opportunity, the direction, and the reasons to go for it themselves. Leaders may serve, but servants never lead.

Fast-Forward Leadership

During the Allied invasion of Europe in World War II, *pathfinders* were parachutists dropped days in advance of airborne assaults to guide the troops who were to follow. To find Pathways and to lead others through them is the duty of today's organizational pathfinders. *To lead* means to guide by going in advance. But prospectors go in advance as well—only they go alone. The difference is that leaders, or pathfinders, guide others.

Leading is no longer the duty of a chosen few, of those at the top of our organizations. It's needed at all levels and in all groups. Groups can be pathfinders too, when they embark on new projects, embrace new processes, and accept the challenge of change. Every contemporary organization has its future at stake. And every organization, no matter how large or small, must stake its future on individuals—leaders, the ones who "guide by going in advance." The ones who will make it into the future also let leadership cascade downward and outward—so that others can lead as well. They know that *to lead* is to leverage excellence—to multiply its benefits throughout their companies. In those excellent companies, you'll find the following techniques at work, everywhere.

1. *Pull, don't push.* Leaders stay in the front, showing others how to approach problems and opportunities. They never win by commanding from the rear. They rely on example, not

threat or control. They know that "you can't push a string": It must be pulled.

2. *Earn trust.* Trust is growing in importance as an essential ingredient in the management of organizations, no matter what their size or role. It cannot be bought, ordered, or assumed. Trust must be earned. This means honesty, dignity, and respect for others are inseparable from leadership.

3. *Give general goals and specific praise.* To lead is to empower others to reach new heights. Constraining or prescriptive rules don't work. And general, nonspecific praise is no help. Let others improvise in finding pathways to excellence, and when they're found, demonstrate specific, detailed encouragement and praise. Publicly celebrate accomplishment.

4. *Encourage difference and similarity.* Tolerate and respect individual differences, but create similarity of goals. Different skills and abilities make a group effective and resilient. Different objectives make it a mob.

5. *Expect excellence.* It won't occur unless you expect it and demonstrate it. Low expectations are self-fulfilling. Keep stretching.

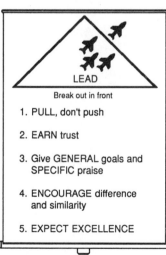

LEAD

Break out in front

1. PULL, don't push

2. EARN trust

3. Give GENERAL goals and SPECIFIC praise

4. ENCOURAGE difference and similarity

5. EXPECT EXCELLENCE

Barriers to Breaking Out in Front

Why isn't everyone a leader, a pathfinder? Is it because a special gift is required, or that there is only room in most companies for just a few? Or is it because to lead is to take chances, to expect the most from yourself, and to be prepared to live with the consequences? This last explanation seems more to the point: We place huge obstacles in front of potential leaders. We want leadership, but the sad fact is we also want its opposites: *compliance, contentment, control.*

Success has its price. So do excellence and leadership. Only those prepared to pay are entitled to the term *leader*. Only those willing to live without the barriers to leadership can pursue it. Here are some of those barriers. We create them—we can knock them down. We can have leaders, but only if we're ready for them.

1. Depending on the Top. We need leaders at all levels, in all positions, and at all times. "One good person" helps, but that isn't enough. You can't get instant leadership throughout an organization by buying the talents of one executive at the top. All of us face uncertainty, multiple options, and tests of our ability to adapt daily. All of us need leaders—close to the action. Leaders at all levels, in all positions, at all times.

2. Fear of Criticism. To guide by going in advance is to take chances and criticism by those who don't. Leading companies are often envied, even hated (especially by their competitors). But they are always respected. If you want to avoid criticism, I'll give you three simple, surefire techniques: (1) *Think nothing,* (2) *Feel nothing,* (3) *Do nothing.*

3. Being a Spectator. Leaders don't watch, command from the rear, or control from above. They don't spectate, they participate. And they don't allow anyone to sit on the bleachers and watch. If you want to be a spectator, buy stock in the company—then stand aside and let others lead it.

4. Love of Control.   Leading means empowering others, not controlling them. It means encouraging, allowing, and equipping others to do their best. It doesn't mean "keeping them from doing wrong." It means "leading them to what's right." Leaders build commitment, not control.

5. Acting Like an Island.   Today's organizational challenges can't be met by isolated individuals, no matter how good they are. Their vision, their knowledge, and their enthusiasm must spread. It must be leveraged throughout the group. There is no leader when no one is led.

1. DEPENDING on the top

2. Fear of CRITICISM

3. Being a SPECTATOR

4. Love of CONTROL

5. Acting like an ISLAND

The Final Step

Leading is the final step, the last of our six Pathways and the inevitable one. Looking back, you can see each Pathway pointing in this direction and leading to this conclusion. It's no coincidence that good leaders know how to *Listen*, to pick up on the unexpected, the footfalls of approaching change. They make connections and draw patterns, *Prospecting* among the wealth of sometimes confusing information that impinges on all of us—making sense of the emerging threats and the unformed opportunities. They question the rules of the past, breaking some, bending others, *Innovating* tirelessly to make what isn't yet made. They show motion and action, getting across the thought barrier quickly, and bringing a piece of the future into view.

They're not afraid to try and see, to pretend it's fixed, or to visualize what's around the corner. They know that in the end, leadership is evidenced by outcomes, not by intentions. This drives them to push for results, for intelligent *Responses*. While others are reacting to change, withdrawing into their shells for protection, leaders are extending themselves outwards, leveraging their ideas and energy through others. They become the *Adaptive* force in the organization, the one working against inertia and complacency, helping the group to redefine, reshape, and refocus itself, making it more fit for times of turmoil and what lies beyond them. *Leading*—it's the apex of survival. It's the process of success. It's the treasure at the end of the Pathways. It's the final act of self-preservation and group salvation. It's how you *save yourself*.

PictoGame—Round 6

If you watch others where you work, you'll see examples of good and bad leadership all over the place. Some negative examples are fairly predictable, like a low energy level, hiding from problems and trying too hard to restrict others while ignoring the need to motivate them. But other mistakes are becoming quite common, particularly when you consider the difference between managing and leading. If there is one megamistake, that's it: managing when you should be leading—or the converse, leading when you should be managing (but considering the times, the latter happens much less frequently). Look over the five pictograms here for the Lead Pathway and see if you can determine which mistakes or barriers each represents. You'll find some answers I came up with on page 175.

WHAT'S WRONG WITH THESE PICTURES?

1. _____

2. _____

3. _____

(Continued)

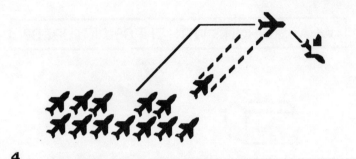

4. _____

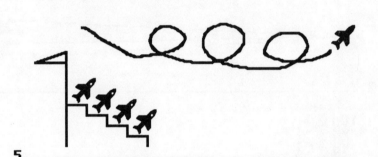

5. _____

PictoGame Answers

Chapter 1: Break the Sound Barrier—The *Listen* Pathway

1. Concentrating exclusively on the main message while ignoring more subtle, perhaps more important ones.

2. Being dedicated to one answer, especially the one from above.

3. Filtering incoming information, as with analysis, judgment, or premature response.

4. Living in a rut, not being open to unexpected sounds.

5. Feeling at the apex of accomplishment when higher, unknown levels await. Success is preventing listening.

Chapter 2: Break the Code to Problems—The *Prospect* Pathway

1. Going for the total answer, the "only way," while ignoring more accessible, easier answers.

2. Going for the fast answer and ignoring better, more appropriate ones.

3. Expecting the complex. Notice the N that is so much closer and easier to get.

4. Being unduly influenced by a negative (such as the word *can't*).

5. Fearing the unknown. The uncertainty surrounding the answer frightens would-be prospectors away.

Chapter 3: Break Away From Convention—The *Innovate* Pathway

1. Experiencing an innovation blocker—punishment for failure, or for simply innovating.

2. Declining innovation because you think someone must have thought of it or done it before.

3. Thinking that only geniuses can innovate, or failing to act stupid.

4. Following the rules and/or being afraid to try.

5. Paralysis by analysis, or studying it to death rather than trying and seeing.

Chapter 4: Break the Speed Limit—The *Respond* Pathway

1. It isn't my job (or it isn't until it's out).

2. Aiming at perfection (or it isn't until it's out).

3. Domino thinking.

4. Not responding fast enough (faster is better).

5. Pursuing the easy no.

Chapter 5: Break Into the Future—The *Adapt* Pathway

1. Waiting until it goes away.

2. Inability to unlearn (or being trapped by the past).

3. Not growing people (or not letting success cascade downward).

4. Unable to unlearn (or failure to erase borders and grow people).

5. Not raising the bar (or accepting success but not excellence).

Chapter 6: Break Out in Front—The *Lead* Pathway

1. Pushing, not pulling (commanding from the rear rather than leading from the front).

2. Love of control (or pushing, not pulling).

3. Not expecting excellence (expecting mediocrity).

4. Not tolerating or welcoming difference.

5. Being a spectator, and watching others lead.

Index